INFOPRENEURS

Infopreneurs

The Hidden People Who Drive Strategic Information Systems

Stephen G. Dance

M

First published 1994 by
THE MACMILLAN PRESS LTD
Houndmills, Basingstoke, Hampshire RG21 2XS
and London
Companies and representatives
throughout the world

ISBN 0-333-60807-0

A catalogue record for this book is available
from the British Library.

Printed in Great Britain by
Ipswich Book Co Ltd
Ipswich, Suffolk

For Diane, Philippa and Lauren

Contents

Acknowledgements

The author and publishers wish to thank the following for permission to reproduce copyright material: CSC Index Limited for a table from one of its Butler Cox Reports; Apple Computer (UK) Limited for an advertisement originally published in the *New York Times,* August 1992; and The Free Press Inc., New York, for a diagram from P. A. Strassman, *Information Payoff,* 1985. Every effort has been made to contact all the copyright-holders, but if any have been inadvertently omitted, the publishers will be pleased to make the necessary arrangement at the earliest opportunity.

1 Corporate IT: Pass or Fail?

THE IMPLIED FAILURE OF IT

Is information technology (IT) suffering from a crisis of confidence? Judging from the results of surveys, press reports, etc., one could be forgiven for thinking so. Perhaps we should not be too surprised for, since the days when computer technology emerged from the confines of academic research, computers, and the issues surrounding them, appear to have been a constant 'thorn in the side' of management. Whether the major issue is one of meeting user-requirements, security, meeting implementation deadlines, training, recruiting and retaining skilled staff, containing costs, or simply making the technology work, one or a number of these issues has been proclaimed as the one which requires the undivided attention of management at some time during the history of IT. Whilst other technologies have had a profound and lasting effect in some industry sectors, IT seems to remains a constant issue to all types of business, large or small.

However, the issues that face IT today are subtly, yet profoundly, different from many of the previous 'hot potatoes' which have been presented to management. Previously management has struggled to come to grips with the technology in terms of its drastic effect on organisational and operational activities.

The major issue which tends to occupy the attention of most boards in major companies today is not one of their ability to deploy IT within their organisation. Most major institutions in the public and private sectors do make considerable use of IT (or at least it accounts for a significant proportion of their cost base). Consequently, they have learned – sometimes the hard way – the implementation aspects of IT. Only the extremely faint-hearted and inexperienced IT-users would shy away from a project because of a lack of faith in their abilities to build and implement a given IT initiative. The question that is now being asked is 'Does it really make any difference to our overall performance?' IT now represents a significant proportion of the overheads of any major company, and executives are now beginning to question whether any tangible contribution to overall corporate performance is being generated.

Many chairmen and boards of directors are viewing their IT function as a bottomless pit into which they are constantly pouring money. What may have been perceived as an initial purchase has turned out to be nothing more than a small holding deposit which demands ever-increasing annual increments. This is paradoxical, since it is the continual penetration of IT into nearly every aspect of corporate life that has heightened awareness not only of its existence and potential, but also of its cost. This leads us to a second paradox; many managers feel that IT could do much more for their company, yet the precise applications to deliver quantifiable benefit appear elusive even to define. Coupled with the complexity of determining the tangible contributions of IT, many managers are feeling trapped; to invest ever-increasing levels of capital into IT becomes difficult, but to be without IT would be unthinkable.

The Panacea that Never Materialised

Looking back over the years, so many of the much-heralded new initiatives seem to fail to live up to expectations. Whether this is due to suppliers' hype or over-optimistic expectations on behalf of the users is difficult to determine. What is apparent is the degree of mounting scepticism and growing disenchantment and, indeed, exasperation. Everything, it seems, turns sour.

It would be inappropriate for us to construct a 'rogues gallery' of IT products that failed to live up to their initial promise at this stage, particularly when the purpose of this book is to put forward principles and concepts of realising satisfactory returns on IT investment. But with the recent moves to measure retrospectively the contribution of IT to business performance the results have been inconclusive. Also they have not been confined to any one particular technology and seem to underline further the difficulties many companies have in obtaining quantifiable business improvement via IT investments.

Development lead times, fulfilling users' functional requirements and meeting project deadlines have, for many years, been major issues to both users and developers alike. The software industry was not slow to see the business potential of providing products to solve these issues. Consequently IT managers were bombarded with products to assist and promote increased productivity in the analysis, design and programming phases of systems development. Over the years we have seen the introduction of new techniques, methodologies and software products which have claimed to undertake one or more of the tasks of systems development more thoroughly, more quickly or with greater flexibility and responsiveness than ever before. Each product in its turn has claimed to project corporate systems development into a braver new world of user-satisfaction and computer-effectiveness than could ever have been previously contemplated. To the practitioner in IT, the potential of these products, many marketed by world leaders, the benefits were obvious; the new methodologies were closely aligned to the corresponding technologies in use and in later years the methodologies themselves were imbedded in impressive software products (i.e. Computer-Aided Systems Engineering). The new software products such as relational databases and fourth-generation languages offered obvious benefits by automating huge chunks of the programming task. Corporate Data Processing (DP) departments too, were quick to realise the potential benefits of these products and submitted convincing proposals to implement the new tools. 'Any system, any time, anywhere' became the clamour of the IT department. Management, too, was impressed by the potential payback of such tools and justified the expenditure on the basis of reduced development lead times, reduced backlog of systems awaiting development and lower software maintenance costs.

Yet, in late 1990, Butler Cox issued their report 'Trends in Systems Development', which contained a number of startling revelations as recorded in their PEP Database. Statistics were showing that there had been no appreciable gains in developer productivity or application quality, so despite the commitment and investment in new methodologies and software products, very little appeared to have changed.

But it is not just the IT practitioners whose vision of the future appears somewhat out of focus; even the businessmen have failed to make IT reach its targets. In the late 1980s, the management gurus of Harvard Business School issued a report which explained in detail how a number of leading American companies had achieved results superior to those of their competitors by the innovative use of information technology. 'IT for competitive advantage' became the proclamation to all of those who were prepared to listen. Whether you needed to increase market share, obtain cost advantage or open up completely new markets, IT could do it. Executives and company directors all over the world were urged to increase their IT budgets substantially, consultants criticised management for not spending enough and warned of corporate fates worse than death if IT budgets were not doubled or trebled.

By 1988 there were some twenty-two methodologies available (for a fee) which gave step-by-step instruction on how to get 'competitive edge' from the company computer. Unfortunately, some time after, all went quiet – because it did not work. Emulating the efforts of the previous paragons of IT virtue was not as easy as it had at first appeared. In the absence of tangible improvements in the 'bottom line' executive attention turned to cost. Having loosened the corporate purse-strings to purchase hardware/software etc., any improvements which had been achieved were not readily quantifiable. All that the corporate balance sheets showed was that IT costs had increased and little else had changed. Company management suddenly realised that despite the increasing amounts of capital being poured into IT, this was not being translated into improved financial results or business performance. This disappointing state of affairs brings us more or less up to date as management asks itself 'Where is the payoff in IT?' This issue was eloquently put by Sir Denys Henderson, Chairman of ICI:

> I still worry enormously, both about the amount we spend on IT and the increasing difficulty of justifying that expense in terms of the bottom line. In the end, I think that this will work to the disadvantage of the suppliers of hardware, software and systems because simply to say 'Can you afford not to spend when you look at your competitors?' or, alternatively, 'There is a hidden commercial advantage which is unquantifiable' will, quite frankly, not be enough in future...

A sobering thought indeed. I do not believe that we have arrived at this stage because of incompetence on the part of end-users nor by developers and/or suppliers deliberately misleading their customers. IT never was nor will be a universal panacea for all corporate problems. Despite the few success stories, the past years have demonstrated that buying in IT as an act of faith will not of itself guarantee business success.

Following its pervasive march into most aspects of corporate life, IT has come out of the back room and into the boardroom and is thus more visible, and with that visibility comes accountability. Additionally, as technology has become cheaper and as more products are introduced into the market-place, IT is pervading almost every aspect of 'work' as we know it. The overriding issue facing many companies today is that of knowing where and how to apply IT within their organisation. 'Failure' in this context is not so much one of a disfunctioning system as a case of lost opportunity; innovative IT solutions elude these companies not because they adopt an incorrect solution, but because many are not even aware that an opportunity is presenting itself.

WHY WE FAIL TO EXPLOIT INFORMATION TECHNOLOGY

Why do so many of our IT systems fail to deliver? Why do organisations invest in systems which, in retrospect, make no tangible contribution to corporate performance despite their earlier promise? On the surface of it, the roots of the problem appear technique-oriented. Hence, managements tend to focus on introducing new and 'better' techniques in the area of project management, new systems development tools, new methodologies, etc. These, however, often prove as disappointing as the problems they were introduced to solve.

It is my experience that the problem lies not within technical issues, but in the more subtle areas of change management. It is primarily a problem in the way the organisation itself works, rather than being the wrong choice of technique or method. Failure to exploit IT is not an issue of technical competence (however, technical competence is mandatory to implement any given solution). It is primarily caused by organisations which as a whole find it either difficult or impossible to operate from, or even envisage, new ways of doing things.

The Common Causes of Failure

If failure is measured in terms of either failure to meet a specification or widespread malfunction which causes total inoperability, few IT systems are true failures. Failures such as these do occur, of course, and are spectacular when they happen. The most common failure, however, is a failure to improve substantially on what has gone before. What tends to happen with major IT projects is that their outcome is often disappointing, failing to live up to its earlier expectations. System proposals such as 'improved efficiency', 'improved competitiveness' or 'better information' hardly ever seem to make the transition from outline specification to an operational system. Despite the investment and organisational commitment, the systems, though implemented, seem to make little difference to the way the organisation operates. The major reason for this is that many organisations resist change, not actively, but passively. Whilst there may be general acceptance of the need for change, the nature of many organisations causes them to resist change unconsciously – even when they believe they are changing. This resistance, though passive and often unintentional, presents itself in several ways.

Blind faith investment

Many managements have adopted a 'blind faith' approach to IT investment and have pursued a strategy of 'the more you buy, the better it will be'.

The illusion of creating sweeping change by implementing large projects has fuelled the false expectations of IT in many boardrooms. The principal failure in many institutions has been their failure to learn from previous mistakes. Rather, they have tended to pin their hopes on the latest technology or technique as the ultimate panacea to correct the previous ills. As with most professions, IT is an evolutionary rather than a revolutionary activity. Huge projects tend to create huge problems.

IT is still a relatively new corporate function when compared with the familiar 'old guard' of personnel, accounting, marketing, etc. Therefore, like it or not, mistakes are bound to have occurred; misunderstanding business requirements, investing in the 'wrong' technologies, and projects being allowed to run out of control are all part of a sometimes painful learning curve. Much of the reticence of managers to invest further in IT is caused by these earlier mistakes. Quite simply, they do not want to get burned again. But the greatest barrier of all is that of unfulfilled expectations. However, in many cases, the original expectations and perceptions were ill-conceived and unjustified. The predictions of benefits were based on a misunderstanding of the forces of internal change and of the nature of IT itself. Too many organisations and individuals within them believe that IT itself is the force of change – which is fallacious.

The reason why so many executives question the pay-off from IT is because the nature of the pay-off is just not understood. IT does not pay off, or does not *appear* to pay off in many organisations for three major reasons:

- The manner in which the implementation and change in the management process is conducted.

- Unrealistic expectations of benefits.
- The manner in which 'value' will be added is either misunderstood or not known.

Because of this, further investment is questioned and value is difficult to measure because management are looking in the wrong place.

Big is not beautiful

Generally speaking, big projects mean big risk. Whilst the big resources are required to fund a big failure, at the 1991 COMPACS conference in London, a consultant from KPMG-Peat Marwick demonstrated an interesting correlation that the bigger the company, the greater the propensity to initiate a mega-flop!! Large companies generate unnecessarily complex systems in order to reflect their excessively complex structure and systems. Many large projects have faltered at the outset because of the sheer size of the requirements and the overpowering complexity of the data structures required to support the unnaturally complex organisational structure.

Many systems investments have embraced an excessively complex organisation and sought to maintain it in its current form. The value of systems such as these will be both marginal and difficult to measure. Systems such as these, from a value-added perspective, are doomed from the start. A system which preserves an inefficient process cannot add value, the best it can do is grease the complex system of cogs and wheels so that they run a little more smoothly.

In *Thriving on Chaos*, Tom Peters raises the issue of the 'American penchant for giantism'. He points to the way that misdirected emphasis on being the biggest has created giant organisations with lumbering, inefficient systems. These giant companies are also giant computer-users whose systems reflect the user-organisation's structural complexity.

It is this organisational complexity which fuels 'mega projects', and even when they are successfully implemented, the value added is difficult to measure. The major reason is, of course, that the functions and systems which were the target of automation were not adding any value in the first place. Computerise a bureaucracy and all you will achieve is a computerised bureaucracy.

Any company contemplating a major systems implementation would do well to challenge its current systems before spending one penny more on IT. Asking questions like 'Why are we doing this?' 'Why do we do it this way?' and 'Can this be simplified?' before automating will reap larger benefits than applying IT to preserve the current inadequacies and inefficiences.

The cost labour trade-off does not work

There is mounting evidence that investing in technology to shed labour cost is a flawed calculation. Whilst jobs may be shed, other functions spring up which require skilled labour to perform them.

This point has been broadly made by Drucker, who cites the hospital sector as an example. As an ever-increasing amount of technology is introduced into the health-care environment, staff requirements are going up because of the specialist skills needed to operate the equipment. The US Bureau of Statistics figures highlighted by Paul Strassman in 'Information Payoff' seem to substantiate that a similar phenomenon is also occurring in IT (see Figure 1.1). This graph clearly shows that as the requirement for 'other' workers declines, the requirement for information workers increases. What is particularly interesting about these figures is that the trend lines are so complementary; the decline on the one line is matched by an equal incline on the other.

This indicates, of course, that there is an equal though opposite shift in labour requirements. IT may be eradicating certain categories of labour but it is creating a requirement for other skills in the process. Therefore, whilst certain clerical tasks are being automated, there is a consequent shift in labour requirement for programmers, operators and analysts to develop and maintain the resulting systems. Moreover, these staff are more expensive in every sense than their 'unskilled' predecessors. In addition to the salary premium commanded, the 'support overhead' required in order to allow

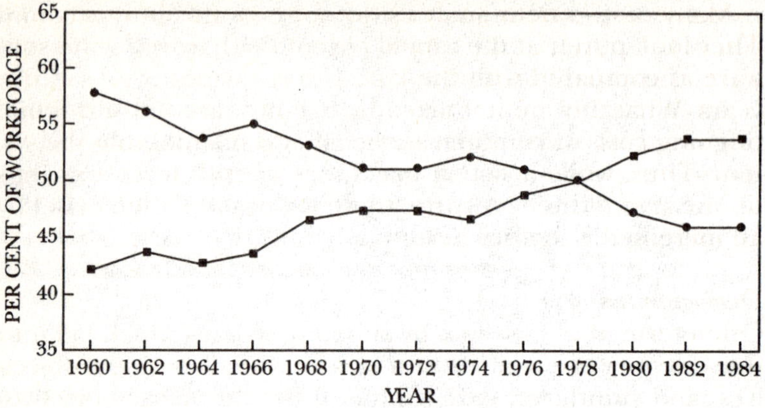

Key: —■— Information workers —●— All other workers.

Source: Adapted from P.A. Strassman, *Information Payoff* (New York: Free Press, 1985).

Figure 1.1 Information workers versus all others

these individuals to operate in an effective and controlled manner is far greater. For instance, a typical programmer will require the following in order to operate effectively:

- Tools (workstation, software utilities and development products)
- Support personnel (word-processor (WP) systems, secretaries, computer operators, software librarians, etc.)
- Training (new products, new development techniques, business orientation).

Investing in IT to reduce organisational cost is more likely to raise the overall cost structure – at best it will remain the same but with different constituent parts. Once an organisation invests capital to create an IT resource, it also creates an almost self-perpetuating requirement for further capital. IT becomes part of the very fabric of the enterprise and represents a vital part of the costs of being and staying in business.

Many cost–benefit analyses do not take this into account. They look purely at the capital cost of the hardware and software as compared with the labour-cost savings over, say, five years. What they do not take into account are the additional ongoing costs of running, servicing and maintaining the system. Thus, while a system may indeed result in cost savings in one area of the enterprise these savings are often offset by an increased cost elsewhere.

Over-engineering

Often termed as 'paralysis by analysis', systems which fall into this category are typified by a lack of overall business objectives, and protracted design phases. Because clear objectives and relative priorities have not been clearly stated, the project becomes involved in incorporating the most trivial of requirements and providing functions to anticipate almost every business eventuality.

Systems which fall into this category when (and if) they are finally implemented are often cumbersome and unwieldy, suffering from 'functional overload'. Because of the 'all things to everyone' approach, users become deterred by the daunting task of coming to terms with the system and it quickly becomes apparent that only a small subset of the systems facilities are used to any great extent. Because of the over-indulgence during the design phase, the system can become unresponsive to change and expensive to maintain. Valid and necessary adaptations of the system may require a protracted process of change management in order to integrate new adaptations into an already overcomplicated, yet underused, architecture.

In situations such as these, rather than obvious loss, the user organisation incurs unnecessary additional overhead in both the development and 'live' stages of the system. Wastage of resource is incurred during the analysis phase by both IT staff and users in the specification and ratification of functions which have little or no business payoff. Training takes longer, and the users' learning curve is protracted, so that exploitation of any real benefit contained within the system takes longer to come on-stream. Finally, the maintenance effort becomes complex and protracted. Costs are incurred here in respect of the additional maintenance overhead required as compared with a simpler design, and in lost opportunity. As maintenance cost increases, so the potential of payback from enhancements is further decreased. Therefore, the adaptation cost could overrule the business rationale for implementing the enhancement.

Why then do we over-engineer a system? Over-engineering a system is not something that is done deliberately. It is the result of building in organisational bad habits particularly those such as excessive compartmentalisation and specialisation. Many organisational structures are built around management paradigms created for the industrialised society. They are typified by multi-levelled hierarchy and 'production-line' techniques for programming work. Since IT is generally recognised to be capable of supporting new organisational models and working practices, it would seem appropriate to challenge current methods and organisational structure before embarking on the development of a new system. Unfortunately, only a handful of organisations do this. Most assume, however, that the purpose of the system is to mimic what is currently done and that the benefit will come from doing it faster. Consequently, many of the marginal activities, contrived specialisations and organisational compartments become incorporated within the system. The result is a large, complex system which makes little tangible improvement in the organisation. The marginal activities which have grown up over the years, rather than being challenged are incorporated into the system. The outcome of the 'new' system is therefore merely an alternative means of preserving the old inefficiencies.

Too much too soon

Any systems-driven change in an organisation creates a training requirement for the users of the new system. The more extensive the change, then the greater is the need for the retraining of those affected by it. Large-scale change has another problem however, and that is the question of just how much change can be absorbed at any one time.

When cut-over to a major system is conducted over a short period, its users are exposed to an intense requirement to cope with, rather than exploit, the system. The nature and intensity of the change is so dramatic that core competences must be quickly established so as to keep the company operations going. Thus, after the post-implementation mountain has been climbed and the pain has subsided, the organisation breathes a sigh of relief, and looks forward to 'getting back to normal'. Large implementations can create an organisational stress level of such magnitutude that coping with the system becomes the ultimate objective rather than exploiting it further. The organisation ends up with nothing more than an alternative method of doing what it did before, rather than an improved one. The sheer scale of the change has diverted attention from exploitation of the new system to survival of the company.

Failure to build on the existing application base

Most firms fail miserably in exploiting the potential of the systems they have before they invest in new ones. When new systems are implemented, many organisations consider that the job is done and that the system is now in maintenance mode. However, the reality is that the job is nowhere near finished – all that has happened is that a foundation has been laid on which they must build.

Many of the technologies available today, particularly those associated with information management (i.e. query languages, databases, PC packages) provide potential rather than a specific functional capability. And although these may be used to implement a particular application, a significant amount of unexploited potential will remain lying latent. Since it is not possible to anticipate each and every potential use of a system prior to implementation, there needs to be an ongoing, post-implementation focus on building on what is already done.

This therefore implies a requirement for continual training and evaluation in the use and capabilities of new systems and technologies. It also implies that new attitudes are required, so that certain technologies are considered as new facilities which must be exploited and built upon over time. Hence an organisation will need to instigate processes which incorporate ongoing training and orientation and which encourage the further exploitation of new systems. The post-implementation period of any new system is not the part where 'the fat lady sings'; it is merely the beginning. During this stage an organisation should be continually learning to respond to new IT facilities and this can only be achieved by providing the workforce with the capability to respond.

Investing in marginal activities

Installing IT systems into organisational functions or activities whose value is not known or is uncertain is another sure-fire way of making benefits elusive. Conversely, investing in IT (rather than allocating capital) because progress has made the particular item a 'standard' is the type of expenditure which will never show a return – no matter how hard you look.

No use of IT provides a better example of this than 'office automation' in all its various guises. Office automation was set to revolutionise the way offices ran. Personal workstations, networks, electronic mail (E-Mail), personal databases, notebooks, diaries, calendars, personal organisers, were hailed as innovations which would raise office productivity to heights which previously could only have been imagined. In all but a few cases this has not happened. Offices, by and large, are the same as before – but have a great deal more equipment in them than they used to. And what of the paper mountain? Is it shrinking? Not according to recent data from the USA, where it is actually growing.

The paperless office is now generally regarded as myth; few managers, consultants (and, indeed, vendors) believe it is a reality. Office automation started on a false premise of 'install the technology and the people will follow'. The truth is that people prefer paper and studies have shown that there are important physiological reasons for this. The first is that it has been established that the fine nerve-endings in our fingers have a relationship with our optical nerves. This is translated into far higher levels of cognition when the two are combined in, say, holding and reading a piece of paper. Take the touch factor away and cognition levels and speed of information assimilation take a massive dive. Recent studies have also identified that there is also a relationship between cognition levels and screen resolution. The higher the screen resolution, the more of the information shown on it is understood and retained. Many aspects of office automation therefore are at odds with very deep-seated natural reactions.

It is probably this which is behind the recent statement of Rank Xerox Corporation that 95 per cent of office records are still stored on paper rather than electronically. Either consciously or subconsciously the average office worker has expressed the preference or, perhaps, the need to work with a physical medium rather than its electronically abstracted counterpart.

Highly compartmentalised, specialised organisations will have many complex and convoluted communications to achieve anything. Hence, office work is often the result of this complexity and bears little resemblance to its' underlying purpose. They are likely to spend more time communicating to each other what they have done and what they intend to do rather than actually doing it. Compartmentalisation and specialisation of function in the office is a direct descendant of the manufacturing management theories, built on the principle of maintaining small independent units undertaking simple and repetitive tasks. In such a culture efficiency gains can be implemented paying little regard to other functions within the overall process. This works well in a linear-process environment, but not in an office environment which is basically an intercommunicating network.

As an organisational network grows in size and complexity, so the overall effectiveness of the individuals contained within it decreases. In other words, the value they add becomes marginal and ever more difficult to determine. Therefore it necessarily follows that the value of investing IT in these functions will be difficult to determine. Executives who become concerned with personal computer (PC) expenditure and office automation cost often ask (sometimes publicly) 'What is the value of this?' In the majority of cases they probably know the answer – none. Replacing a secretary's typewriter with a W/P station or a PC will not make her measurably more productive. It does not matter how many more memos, meetings, etc., the secretary can cope with nor, indeed, how many additional tasks the technology enables her to cope with. The cost of the secretary does not change. No matter how efficient she becomes, her activities are marginal as to whether the company makes a profit or not. It may make life a little more convenient or comfortable but the value to the organisation of the work conducted by the secretary will remain the same. What does not remain the same are the costs of providing her with IT:

- The work-station costs more than a typewriter.
- The PC costs more than a typewriter.
- The central system or Local Area Network (LAN) server requires capital expenditure to procure it and run it, and an administrator for day-to-day operation.
- The secretary has to be trained (and then finds her new-found skills give her the opportunity to command a premium salary!)

Although I do not intend to inspire a Luddite revolution arguing that all office automation equipment should be piled high and burned, there is a case for pragmatism. The point is that many functions within an organisation, though necessary for it to function, add only marginal value to the bottom line. Consequently, IT investment in these areas must by definition generate equally marginal returns. Office technology implemented in this manner will not obliterate bureaucracy; it will merely become integrated within it.

Process takes precedence over purpose

Many new systems fail to deliver benefits because they have concerned themselves with automating a process at the expense of re-evaluating the process against the purpose. Automation of a process primarily concerns itself with the 'how' of the process rather than the 'what'. Consequently, the value of the function becomes overlooked as the process of automating it becomes preoccupied with the manner in which it is performed.

Systems developed in this manner become excessively process-orientated as all involved focus their attention on making the system 'fit in' with what is currently done. Any organisation or department currently considering a major IT project will do well to evaluate what it is currently doing and why it is doing it that way. Before committing any resources to IT, it should consider whether the function could be conducted more effectively or simplified by procedural change or re-organisation. As mentioned previously, many office procedures are the result of organisational design rather than having any other deeper justification for their existence.

Customer service considerations

These can often be compromised when an organisation becomes so preoccupied with containing costs that the systems implemented actually work to the disadvantage of the customer base. At its worst, initiatives such as these can actually erode a competitive position.

For instance, centralisation of order-processing and acceptance has, in some industries, provided considerable savings of staff-related costs. However, in organisations where the core business is distributed and customers are actually serviced locally, this approach could work to the detriment of the organisation as a whole. For example, a company which has built up a reputation for being able to satisfy last-minute orders from its customers may have a commercial edge over its competition. Because of this it may be in a position to charge a premium price for its goods and services. Unless the centralised function is capable of empowering local management with the authority to make necessary last minute rescheduling decisions, this competitive edge may be lost.

Thus, a company which creates this type of situation may, in fact, lose out even if the system helps in achieving the required cost reductions. This is because the 'value chain' has been re-configured by the system, and in so doing has removed the 'value added' capability which previously gave the organisation competitive edge. Consequently, cost-savings may be achieved at the expense of customers and lost revenue.

Vague goals

Goal-setting, management by objectives, and other related techniques have, for some considerable time, been used as tools with which to manage performance, productivity and overall corporate goals. Goal or objective setting, done unambiguously, is an invaluable tool for stating requirements. It serves to concentrate focus on the major issues and acts as a unifying influence on all involved in a particular activity.

In a profession which is so 'specification bound' as IT, one could expect that the goal-setting expertise of those involved should be second to none. However, one of the major reasons why many IT projects do not deliver tangible returns is because they do not satisfy an overall organisational objective. The initial rationale for a development initiative often becomes forgotten as both users and developers become more and more involved with the minutiae of specification and acceptance activities. In some cases the development methods themselves become the major force behind the project as the members of the project team become more and more involved with complying with the dictates of the methodology rather than delivering the necessary functionality.

In other cases, the organisational objectives of the new system are so vague and/or ambiguous that the project is doomed from the start. A particularly good example of this is given in Tom Gilb's 'Software Engineering Management':

> The key business attributes of the new system...is to give an appropriate level of customer service in supplying products, to have an appropriate stockholding consistent with that and to have a more flexible and efficient utilisation of resources leading to increased profitability

What was this company trying to do? In fact it was trying to shave $400 million off its overheads! This is obviously an extreme example of an ambiguous requirements statement, but similarities exist in major development projects which are running today. With such unclear targets, no system will ever deliver – except by luck. At this level, the ball is firmly in the management's court. The objectives of the system and the functions required to generate the required benefits must be stated in a clear, unambiguous and quantifiable manner. In later stages, management must ensure that all those involved in the development remain focused on these objectives.

IS THERE A THREAT?

Should we be worrying about this at all or are we trying to make a silk purse out of a sow's ear? The cynicism with which many senior managers apparently view IT would seem to enforce this view. Perhaps we should adopt the attitude that information technology is purely an overhead and should be managed as such. In the short term, life would most certainly be easier – simply attack the overhead and give ourselves a pat on the back when we have made some savings.

Unfortunately, neither life nor business is that simple. No one won an Olympic medal by dropping out of the event. And a similar analogy exists with corporate IT. In 1984, A.T. Kearney reported that companies which lagged behind in their use of information technology 'are six times more likely to have a poor financial performance within their sector than companies leading in IT'. Even if we do not know exactly how IT makes a difference, it certainly seems to do no harm. This is further enforced by Kearney's observation that the gap between leaders and laggers is growing.

The threat, then, is that with under-investment or with low levels of commitment to IT, organisations run the risk of becoming uncompetitive. Although we cannot directly correlate IT-usage to corporate performance, taking it out of the corporate architecture would appear to invite inferior performance.

A MANAGEMENT ISSUE – NOT A TECHNICAL PROBLEM

Getting IT to work for the benefit of the organisation is an issue for managers, not for the developers. Any manager at any level in an organisation is responsible for the utilisation, deployment and direction of the resources at his disposal and IT is but one of them. The problem which most managers face is that the tools and techniques with which to manage the IT resource effectively are not clearly defined. What makes one company 'good' at managing information is a difficult thing to determine. There appears to be no real formula for success.

However, persevere we must. As the economies of the western hemisphere increasingly rely on revenue generated from services rather than manufactured products, the effective use of IT will increasingly become a major factor of corporate performance.

2 The Information Resource

Why *is* information a resource? And, perhaps more importantly, why has it recently become so? The past ten years or so, in business and information technology (IT) terms, are notable for a significant change in attitude towards IT. No longer seen as a purely back-room activity, information-processing has been demonstrated as a tool for improving business performance. It can be used not just for automating 'behind the scenes' activities, but to provide new services, adding value to existing ones, improving knowledge of the customer base and improving the speed and quality of business decisions.

Nonetheless, except for a few notable case studies, returns on investment in this resource have proved both disappointing and elusive for many companies.

The problem for many companies is that they are not sufficiently aware of the relevance and possible application of information to their business to make full use of it. Their understanding of its relevance in enabling them to manage their business more effectively is not sufficiently well-developed to allow them to exploit the information available to them for the benefit of their business. The central issue is that far too many managers have not realised that fundamental changes have occurred within their organisations and that a whole raft of possibilities and capabilities are now available to them. Information and IT provide a potential capability to change radically the way we conduct, manage and organise our business. The difficulty faced by the majority of executives is not in their understanding of technology. A mental block exists in terms of how and where to look in order to identify information and applications which will improve the overall effectiveness of the organisation. Yet every so often a handful of individuals, spurred on by both vision and intuition hit the elusive target and develop an innovative application which creates a radical and beneficial change within their company.

THE HISTORY OF THE INFORMATION RESOURCE

Information, like oil, has always been a resource. But like oil, the employment of information as a resource has been dependent on two things:

1. An understanding of its capability to contribute in providing a solution or part of a solution.
2. The existence of appropriate technology initially to release the resource and subsequently to refine and distribute it.

As IT has developed, the potential to capture, store and employ information in the pursuit of managing and conducting our business has correspondingly increased. Over the course of time the increasing flexibility and versatility of IT has created new information flows and repositories. What was once an inert mountain of paper is now a stream of potentially manageable information, which may be subsequently distilled into knowledge. Information now flows from the 'front line' of the business to the decision-makers faster than ever before. Information which never before existed in manageable form can now be captured, assimilated and evaluated. The real question that executives should be asking themselves is not 'what should I do with the information I get?', but 'what information do I need to make informed decisions that will increase business performance?'

The early days of IT were typified by applications whose sole purpose was to improve efficiency. These applications were directed at low-level record-keeping, principally the automation of the accounting function. Computers were more economic than an army of clerks – they did not get bored with repetitive functions, did not take holidays and were less prone to illness. At this time, the concept of using IT for competitive advantage, or indeed any strategic advantage, had not yet been formed. Systems were just one tool in the hands of the executive to manage the company's cost structure. Applications of IT were therefore focused on replacing labour, rather than generating knowledge. The only strategic perspective that could be adopted was on the nature and the quantity of the technology to be applied.

These early days of computers allowed only one small piece of the organisation's information 'jigsaw' to be held in digital form. Now huge parts of the overall picture can be held – and used. The old accounting systems, used to record what had happened, provided a crucial yet incomplete view of the organisation. Only limited decisions could be made on the basis of the information provided and little knowledge of the overall operational behaviour of the company, its customers and markets was conferred. Employed principally as a matter of record and to provide clerical efficiency gains, these systems informed executives of *what* had happened but not *why*.

For almost 2000 years, paper has been the principal means by which to record, store and transport information. Paper, however, is an inflexible and bulky medium. When information has been recorded on paper for one purpose it becomes extremely difficult to use that information for any other purposes. The manner of storage has thus been a constraint on the inherent flexibility of information. It is this historical constraint which has denied organisations access to their information and their perceptions of its structure. The introduction of computers provided two great steps forward in the field of information management:

1. It provided an alternative to human and mechanical calculating machines in the areas of processing information.
2. It provided an alternative storage medium.

In terms of information-processing the computer was another small step in the progression from the mechanical accounting machine. It merely provided a more efficient alternative. By far the most radical influence of IT lies within its' ability to store and retrieve information digitally. This advance in storage technology with the associated processing logic has increased the accessibility of information by several orders of magnitude. By virtue of this, computer technology not only offered an alternative storage medium to paper, it offered a vastly improved capability to manage the information previously recorded on it.

THE ROLE OF TECHNOLOGY IN EXPLOITING THE INFORMATION RESOURCE

Via IT we have obtained the ability to capture, move, order and share information (both within and outside the organisation). These capabilities have allowed us to learn and know more. The computer has allowed us to assimilate and transfer information at a far greater rate than any other storage medium.

Each advance in the specialist areas of information has either increased capability or reduced the cost of realising that capability:

Communications technology has provided the means whereby information can be delivered quickly from one remote corner of the globe to another.
Storage and graphics technology have increased our ability to store not only textual, character orientated information but also images.
Database software has greatly enhanced our capabilities to re-order existing information, to consider its implications from a different viewpoint and to share it with others.

Perhaps the real advantage of IT is its ability to allow information to be structured and analysed from many different perspectives. The capability to look at the same information and study it and act upon it according to different criteria, to summarise it, compare it and extrapolate interrelationships, has provided us with a panoptic phenomenon. By these capabilities, IT has allowed a vast repository of potential knowledge to be created. This enables individuals to learn new things about their organisation and markets and, if so motivated, to apply them to the benefit of their organisation. But as with an encyclopaedia or a dictionary you have to be searching for an answer in order to find one. The repository of the answer is passive, it cannot anticipate your question or prompt a solution of its' own volition.

ORGANISATIONAL CHANGE AND KNOWLEDGE TRANSFER

IT has the capacity to 'flatten' organisations by removing artificial barriers caused by compartmentalisation and by eradicating the need for various levels of supervision. These effects are a consequence of improved information flows and increased access to information. As a result, more information and faster access to it facilitates knowledge transfer between functions as people see more of an overall process. Large chunks of the organisation are opened up and allow the adoption of different viewpoints and perspectives.

The process of organisational flattening is intrinsically intertwined with the removal of the artificial divisions that exist in many organisations. By making data more accessible, information which was previously ensconced within departmental or individual 'fiefdoms' is now liberated. Prior to the introduction of technology, the presentation of information was inclined towards the support of one particular process or supervisory approach and followed prescribed paths up the organisational hierarchy. With IT the source data becomes both available and flexible and can be used to support several different perspectives.

Introducing technology into any information-processing environment potentially facilitates a change in the behaviour of the underlying information. Manual information-processing systems are inherently inflexible without considerable manpower and effort to effect such a change. IT, in contrast, allows experimentation and knowledge transfer by allowing an 'information entrepreneur' to undertake analytical work which previously would have required an army of clerks. Via his work-station masses of information can be accumulated, structured and analysed.

'UNEXPECTED' BENEFITS

Applying IT has often brought benefits to the user organisation which were not originally planned. In some notable cases they have actually outweighed the originally perceived benefits of the project. The unexpected benefits of IT form an aspect which has risen to prominence in recent years. In fact, 'unexpected' benefits have even been used as an inducement to invest in IT, as if there were some magical property associated with the mere possession of it. To hear some reports, the presence of IT facilities will introduce some form of serendipity within the organisation. These 'unexpected' benefits of IT however are not some kind of post-implementation bonus. They are the result of changed user-perspective in response to a previous IT-driven change. It has absolutely nothing to do with serendipity nor will it be automatically realised. What we are dealing with is the very fundamental process of learning. In this case it is learning new capabilities when our surrounding environment is changed. We are again faced with the rather elusive issue of understanding the behaviour of information and how it can be harnessed when placed in a technological environment.

Case Study: From E-Mail to Competitive Advantage

The concept of an E-Mail network is one which conjures up many images of enhanced office productivity:

removing paper from the system (cost reductions),
reduced lead times of information delivery (improved communication),
the ability to re-use documents (improved information management),

Indeed, the first two benefits – especially the improved communications – were the reason for a British engineering company investing in an E-Mail system. The company in question installed an E-Mail network to improve communication between management and the workforce across a number of sites in the UK. Although this was successful to some extent, the envisaged benefits were not wholly achieved. However, one aspect which was not originally envisaged far outweighed those at first perceived. Because the E-Mail network allowed staff of different departments to communicate with each other quickly and efficiently the company found they were obtaining responses to requests for proposals and quotations far more quickly than before. Because sales, technical and other departments could share information, pass it back and forth, reform it and enhance it, the process of proposal formulation was drastically cut down. Whilst any financial benefit may have been difficult to determine, the company clearly obtained an advantage over its competitors. Its ability to respond quickly to tender invitations was responsible for the company winning several contracts.

The most significant aspect of this example is not that E-Mail or IT can make you more responsive. The real breakthrough is that *the firm realised* how improved information flow provided a new linkage with its business processes which could benefit the organisation. It is the result of seeing new perspectives, learning and opportunism that makes the difference, not necessarily the technology or its original application.

WE PERCEIVE THAT WHICH WE ARE CONDITIONED TO PERCEIVE

The Western countries' knowledge of the extent and behaviour of the solar and celestial system is probably the most extensive of all the countries in the world. This knowledge, allied with the West's knowledge of the various other technologies associated with jet propulsion, physics, etc., has formed the basis for the great advances in space travel which we have witnessed over the past three decades. The West, however, was not always in the lead. In the early fifteenth century, Chinese philosophers and mathematicians had a far more extensive knowledge of the universe than their European counterparts.

One major reason for this was the influence of religion on the thinking of these different peoples. The Buddhist religion, adopted by the Chinese at that time, advocates a lifetime of continual growth in the understanding of self and our place within the vast design of nature. By contrast, in Europe at that time, religious practice was relatively more harsh and dogmatic and in many respects more parochial. Questioning the reason of 'higher order' things was to tread the path of heresy by raising doubt over 'accepted' concepts. Our European ancestors did not look any further than the then-current teachings and explanations available to them.

Thus two different views of the universe emerged. Both had merit and both, depending on the society in which one was born, were correct. As religious tolerance grew and science became acceptable and eventually laudable, so our ancestors' understanding grew. Stimulated by information which showed them a different perspective, encouraged by a society which embraced learning and understanding, knowledge increased.

Our perceptions and understanding of any thing or situation are influenced by three major factors:

- our current knowledge
- our past experience
- the information which is currently available to us

We learn, obtain new perspectives and subsequently apply them when a situation arises that:

- allows us to see something familiar in a different light or as part of a new relationship;
- has a potential 'value' within the sphere of our current activity;
- we feel motivated to take some action upon.

These points indicate why making information more flexible can bring unexpected benefits. By making information more accessible and malleable, different perspectives within a familiar context can be obtained. This process facilitates learning, broadens understanding and encourages the process of innovation.

OPPORTUNISM

Opportunism is the act of capitalising on some unexpected event or occurrence. The use of information is a vital ingredient in any opportunistic course of action. Today's organisations must encourage the concept of 'information opportunism' in order to realise fully the potential within their information systems. Users must be encouraged to probe their information systems across departmental and divisional boundaries, monitor changes within their business environment and assimilate the capabilities and consequences of new technologies.

It is interesting to note how well opportunism has served mankind throughout its short history:

- Penicillin was discovered when bacteria failed to grow on a certain culture which had *accidentally* become contaminated by a mould.
- Synthetic fibres were discovered by the DuPont corporation when a reaction vessel, previously used in unrelated research on polymers, was being cleaned.
- A catalyst required for the production of artificial rubber was discovered when a mercury thermometer was used as a drink stirrer.
- Artificial sweeteners became a reality when a researcher in a different field noticed his cigarette tasted sweet after being left to burn on a laboratory bench.
- X-rays were discovered while conducting research into cathode rays.

All these examples have one thing in common – accident! Whilst they were all working to a common goal, the final goal was realised by an element of luck, or in other terms by an event in some unrelated activity. Perhaps the most interesting are those where something of value emerged as a complete surprise from an initiative that had quite unrelated objectives. To a large degree, they are analogous to the principle of deriving unexpected benefits from IT. All have come from an increase in understanding or knowledge by using information which was previously either hidden or not formally related to the problem at hand. Yet despite the element of luck there was also an intuitive, quantum leap of association which forged a new product or new knowledge.

In a similar way organisations begin to know themselves and their markets better as they probe into the information base and establish new relationships and trends within it. The process of doing so, however, is not so much one of structured deduction but of discovery. Since computer technology has liberated information we have become empowered to learn a great deal more about the relationships within our company and how changes in them affect company performance.

It is pure opportunism followed by analysis that forms so many strategic-systems initiatives. Of the companies studied in Peters and Waterman's book, *In Search of Excellence*, it was established that many of the major initiatives taken by these companies could never have been predicted. Many of the companies' major strategic moves were pure opportunism. From this phenomenon the concept of 'informed opportunism' was formulated; the process of continually searching for new opportunities along a common theme.

Information is not a resource that responds to a rigid protocol or procedure. Its very flexibility and diversity are at odds with such an approach. Before any management philosophy is adopted to exploit information it must be accepted that:

- Information is a flexible and powerful resource; when and how it contributes is not always obvious. Therefore using it strategically can be unpredictable. You cannot predict when a new technology will present a new opportunity or when someone within your organisation will see that opportunity.
- IT is merely a repository and an enabler of information. Technology has no intrinsic value of its own in terms of added business value.
- Information, too, is passive; neither the possession of it nor throwing IT at it will automatically generate benefit.

A different approach to management is now required to exploit fully the opportunities that may be available: firms must learn to consider the contribution which information can make in every facet of its business. Information must be considered in terms of its capability to support operations, convey knowledge and provide new business opportunities.

3 Changing Role, Changing World

The marriage of information with digital computers has spawned profound effects on the way that business is conducted and in the nature of work itself. Technological advances and innovations make computing power increasingly cheap and flexible and ever more-pervasive in the workplace and everyday life. As a consequence information technology (IT) has become ingrained in almost every aspect of work and business activity. This continual proliferation has created an underlying force of continual change within organisations first to adapt to and consequently to exploit the opportunities presented by IT. Organisations and individuals are compelled to change the way they work and are challenged on the way they think about their work.

'The Computer' has been singled out as one of the primary agents of change in the twentieth century. It has changed businesses beyond recognition, spawned new types of business and influences society at large. In order to exploit the opportunities beckoned by this versatile panopticon embedded in silicon companies have recognised that there is a need to develop and nurture new skills, adopt new structures and redefine the role and responsibilities of the IT department. Unfortunately far too many companies accept the need for change but somehow lack the vision and understanding to identify precisely how and to what they should change. The problem is that more than one thing changes: from the way we manage our organisations, the ground-rules for competition and to new products, IT exerts a profound influence on them all.

IT CHANGES THE WAY YOU (AND YOUR COMPETITORS) DO BUSINESS

During its earlier years, IT was considered in a relatively simplistic light, primarily as a replacement for clerical labour. Computers were applied to relatively simple, mechanistic and repetitive tasks such as accounting, payroll and general record keeping. Cost justification was a relatively simple task since the cost of the hardware, software and specialists was offset against the number of clerical jobs that would be 'saved'. Customer interaction with these early systems was low, amounting to, perhaps, a statement or advice slip every so often. The company computer stood isolated in the back room of the company, gobbling up some form of input medium and turning it into pages of printout overnight in a familiar and tightly defined schedule. These early computer systems merely emulated work; each form and report was designed for one purpose and one purpose only. Work, as we then knew it, was simply cross-mapped into a new technological environment. In essence, computer systems merely emulated the human activities associated with information-processing.

However, as the capabilities of the technology increased and improved, more (both in terms of capability and versatility) began to cost less. IT proliferated throughout the workplace, allowing us to select and transfer information hither and thither and generally gave us more of everything. As information became more accessible and access to it was made more flexible, a few forward-thinking companies then began to look at the information held on their computers and began to consider IT in a different light. They saw that the information contained within their systems, coupled with the capabilities of the technology, might contribute, in some way, to the development of their business. It would be difficult to pinpoint precisely when these shifts of perception occurred. But broadly speaking it would seem to coincide with the growing acceptance of on-line systems with database capabilities. These systems introduced end-users to a new and higher level of interaction with the technology and the information contained within it. Information came out of the closet – or at least out of the electronic filing cabinet. In spite of the issues regarding user-friendliness, ergonomics, etc., the on-line systems allowed information to be viewed through different eyes – those of the end-user rather than the technicians. Users conceived of uses for their systems that could never have occurred to the technicians. It became users from all walks of corporate life who, as their confidence and empathy with IT increased, saw new ways to employ technology and information.

The realisation that information can be used for purposes other than telling you what happened yesterday, last week or last month created a significant paradigm shift in a relatively small number of companies. They realised that the ease and speed with which IT managed information allowed it to be sifted and delivered to remote locations. Thus potential opportunities for increasing the speed of response to customers, analysing customer behaviour in great detail and shortening internal supply and communication lines became apparent. This subtle shift of perception permitted them to create new business opportunities and gain an edge over their competitors. In keeping with the flexibility of information liberated by computer technology, the different uses to which information was put under this new paradigm were many.

IT has been employed to forge stronger links with customers and suppliers and even to create new markets (for example, information delivery services). With the advent of smaller and cheaper mini-computers and subsequently even smaller and very cheap personal computers the capital investment considerations changed. Consequently more 'fringe' applications were developed, and as more information became shuffled around and sorted, every once in a while a potential niche market was identified. With the increasing power and capability of computer technology, spiced with some entrepreneurial spirit and vision, it has become possible to package and/or take delivery of information in a manner which can confer a commercial advantage. In many cases the result of these initiatives has been so significant that whole industries have changed the way they work (as competitors attempt to emulate the prime mover), new markets have evolved and different risks have emerged.

But perhaps the most significant issue of all is the overwhelming importance of the marriage between information and IT. As the exploitation of information increases, in the strategic sense, it is thrusting companies into uncharted territories. It is causing them to look outside their traditional product lines in order to increase their business. Who, say, ten years ago, could have predicted that a drugs company or an airline would achieve market dominance because of the way it accepted orders from its customer? But that is precisely what has happened: both McKesson and American Airlines were among the best anyway, but their market dominance was significantly enhanced because their IT systems made it convenient and efficient to do business with them. Call it differentiation, value-added or what you like but it was an information-related service that made American Airlines and McKesson what they were, not just planes or drugs.

This, I believe, is why IT has created so much perplexity in the board rooms; until relatively recently it had no bearing whatsoever on the core business. IT could tell you things about your business but previously had had no part in actually developing it from a strategic viewpoint. Now, it has been demonstrated, IT can make as much of a contribution to a business as a revolutionary new product – providing it is wisely directed. This realisation came as a serious jolt to many directors and chief executive officers (CEOs): they were being beaten by their competitors not because their products were inferior but because of ancillary advantages provided by some innovative use of information technology. Directors and CEOs suddenly realised that they were losing out because their competitors were servicing customers better than they were, managed inventory and manufacturing better than they did and were identifying new markets by using information and IT. By applying IT in critical areas their competitors had acquired ancillary competences which gave a boost to their core business products.

The effect that the exploitation of information has had on business has been as profound as Henry Ford's production-line concept was on the automobile industry, or the discovery of antibiotics to the medical profession. For it has not ended with one final revelation: more and more initiatives and derivatives of the originals have occurred. Thus, in addition to the considerations of advertising, marketing, production and distribution, information has also emerged as a potential tool to shape and monitor corporate performance both strategically and operationally.

THE WIDE-RANGING EFFECTS OF IT DEPLOYMENT

Restructuring Industries

By the automated processing of information, whole industries have been restructured and some have disappeared. IT, by bringing firms closer together, can cut out the 'middleman'. In many industries brokers of services are being cut out as suppliers use IT to allow customers to choose and select their products via point-of-sale terminals.

Significantly Raising Customer Expectations

Federal Express, by the introduction of their COSMOS system were able to lead the market in the parcels delivery service. By being able to fulfil their delivery promise of a '10 a.m. next-day', delivery they have set new standards of performance in this sector. Many of the initiatives taken by Federal Express were associated with internal procedures: that is, the way they processed information which related to the delivery of the parcel. By doing so the parcels spent less time on Federal Express premises and more time in getting to where they were supposed to be. A myriad of technologies were introduced such as the use of hand-held super-tracker terminals to capture bar codes, on-board computers in trucks and a central tracking system in Memphis which tracks the progress of a package as it changes hands in the delivery chain.

The nett result is that Federal Express set the standard for fast, reliable delivery. *It could not have been achieved without forging the perceptive link* between the requirement for speeding up the information collection and dissemination process and the capabilities of information technology.

Identifying Niche Markets

One of the major capabilities of information technology is its ability to categorise, restructure and re-order information in order to identify trends and similarities within a large population of data. For instance, Red Lion Inns – a US hotel chain – used SABRE, the American Airlines reservation system, to identify business travellers who frequently used particular routes. Subsequently Red Lion offered corporates who used these routes non-discounted rates for six months. Although no discounts were offered, predictability of costs was welcomed by many companies. Consequently, Red Lion generated considerable business by identifying this niche and achieved occupancy rates of 3 to 4 per cent above the national average. Three or four percentage points may not seem awe-inspiring, but in the hotel business most costs are fixed, hence most of the revenue generated by that initiative flowed straight to the bottom line.

Adding Value to a Service or Product

Some organisations augment their products by providing a 'value-added' service supported by IT. This type of differentiation can provide a better product fit for a particular niche market, or make it easier to use.

Examples of this are the American Express Corporate Card, which collects business-related expenses and generates statements with additional information. Bank automated telling machines (ATMs) are an example of using IT to extend service hours, thereby making cash-dispensing services easier and more convenient to use. Insurance companies use IT to adjust insurance cover for inflation, automatically increasing annual premiums thus relieving their customers of form-filling and keeping their insurance cover up to date.

Reducing Costs without Sacrificing Quality

The newspaper business in common with many industries, is sensitive to distribution costs. However in the newspaper business distribution may be more expensive than production itself. Since newspapers are, if nothing else, a medium for communicating information there are obvious links with IT. Advances in publishing technology have enabled the publishers of newspapers such as *International Herald Tribune, Financial Times and USA Today* to compose them in one country and then transmit them electronically to other locations to be physically printed – thus eliminating international transportation costs.

Altering the Market Place

If you are a big enough player IT can lock-*in* your current customers and/or lock *out* your competition. Tymshare, a company which provides computer network facilities to many different types of company, runs a specialised network service known as CARDIS. The network is used for the distribution of import/export documents, but is run on behalf of several companies consisting of seven exporters, three ocean carriers and two freight-forwarding agencies. The companies, working in alliance, have created an information cartel, by virtue of which they achieve a speed of response far superior to that of their competitors.

Extending Corporate Boundaries

Networking technology has allowed some companies to extend their systems to their customers' premises. Examples of this are the cash management services operated by a number of major banks, whereby a work-station is situated in a corporate treasurer's office. Using the work-station the treasurer can monitor his cash flow, make payments, check receipts, order foreign currency, make deposits and switch cash between accounts. Industry, too, has examples of systems which cross organisational boundaries to support the supplier/customer relationship. Major automobile manufacturers exchange orders and invoices to support 'just-in-time' manufacturing and speed up the payment process.

Selling/Broking Information

If information is power then it is also a lucrative business. As the requirement for information has become more and more important, particularly in fast-moving financial markets, so a market for information itself has grown. Reuters, formerly a news agency, is now the largest supplier in the world of information to the financial markets. Its core product is purely information distribution.

A more subtle example is that of First Boston Bank which launched the Shelternet service. Shelternet is a mortgage-broking service which links house-buyers, via terminals installed in real-estate-brokers offices, to banks and savings and loans institutions. Although the result is ultimately a mortgage loan, Shelternet provides information which allows house-buyers and lenders to link-up.

All this anecdotal evidence, however is liable to misinterpretation. The above examples are outcomes of a subtle process of learning and strategic conceptualisation. This learning and conceptualisation is in itself the result of the continuing pervasiveness of IT. What is important is not so much the initiative itself but the process of determining what the initiatives should be. Rather than emulating the achievements of a handful of companies, organisations would do better to come to grips with the issues that precluded them from thinking of such an approach. This will not occur until they address the issues of understanding information as a resource and technology as a potential enabler of that resource.

NEW OPPORTUNITIES ARE ACCOMPANIED BY NEW RISKS

The old Jewish proverb 'he who lies down will never fall over' implies that if you never attempt to do anything you are unlikely to incur any of the risks associated with failure. Making significant changes in the way business is conducted brings with it several risks, some of which lie dormant or unseen.

A particularly good example is the concept of 'just-in-time' manufacturing (JIT). Now, while neither information nor IT are the subject of JIT, they enable it by the speedy provision and transfer of information. Many suppliers who supply goods and materials to manufacturers who are using JIT are finding that they are now inheriting much of the inventory-holding costs previously held by their customer. Consequently they are compelled to rethink the way they do business as their customers' use of IT changes the economics of the business.

Being on the outside can also be risky (which smashes the 'do-nothing, no-risk' approach). For instance when Braniff Airlines filed for bankruptcy they blamed the American Airlines SABRE system which, they claimed, eroded their customer base. Not being able to provide IT-supported services which have become a *de facto* industry standard can put a business at a considerable disadvantage if it does not also offer them. Manufacturers who cannot support 'source marking', that is, product bar coding, may find it difficult to move their products as buyer/retailers now rely heavily on this technology. For many retailers bar coding provides the base information which they use to calculate and monitor sales per square foot. If these services cannot be provided, the modern-day imperatives of maintaining what is now mandatory point-of-sale, marketing, sales and inventory information may be so great as to make a potential supplier unattractive.

CREATING NEW STANDARDS OF RESPONSIVENESS

Bar coding technology is a good example of how information can contribute to an organisation's responsiveness: by capturing sales information at the point of sale, customer preferences and consumer trends can be spontaneously tracked, thereby allowing the retailer to invest in fast-moving inventory, thereby maximising capital turnover. The power of information about one thing (sales of goods) to affect something else (consumer trends, capital turnover) is a remarkable phenomenon: change one thing and several related things will change. The trick is to understand the relationships that exist within an organisation's key functions.

IT CHANGES THE WAY IN WHICH ORGANISATIONS PERCEIVE WORK

Most organisations today face a paradox with regard to information management; IT, the very medium which has liberated information, disguises it, and hides it. In consequence, although the information and the facilities to adopt new perspectives on the information are there, few clues are given by the technology as to what they are and where they may be. The onus is still on the user of the information to consider and project new uses for it. Information, viewed outside the perspective of current systems has a highly abstract and an almost transparent nature. It is rather like a fourth dimension, it can be proven to exist but cannot, it seems, be seen, touched or detected unless through especially gifted eyes. Despite the potential power of IT to improve or provide an advantageous commercial position, real mastery of information in these contexts seems as elusive as any Nirvana. The real challenge to today's organisations is not the deployment of technology itself, but that of envisaging the extended or enhanced potential of information and how this might subsequently benefit the business.

The difficulties of working with IT were made clearer by Shoshana Zuboff, a professor at Harvard Business School. In *The Age of the Smart Machine*, Professor Zuboff described and analysed the feelings and responses of workers who had experienced the introduction of IT. The research identified a remarkable similarity between the anxieties of pulp-mill operators and clerks in a bank – despite the obvious differences in the nature of their work. Both groups were concerned with the lack of 'touch' in their work. IT removed an important physical factor of their work, requiring them to work with abstract, mental images. As one put it 'our work floats in space in front of our eyes'. Touch is an important experiential element of learning. By touching something we can, almost unconsciously, learn its relative weight, density, temperature and malleability. Take this away and you have a serious problem of disorientation. With the physical form of information (paper) removed from our grasp, we are forced to work with mental images. Often we have no way of knowing that they are complete or what their relationship is with other areas of the organisation. An important psychological aspect of working with IT is that it is at first highly disorientating. When first introduced to IT-driven change in working practices people are liable to seek out their own comfort-level with the situation. When this has been achieved learning often stops until the next change comes along. Consequently no new uses are found because no one is looking for them – the comfort-level has been found and most are loath to disturb it.

The information contained in many information systems is visible only through the 'windows' and structures provided by the software in the system. Only a handful of people within the organisation (normally the designers of the system) are aware of all the relative connections and dependencies within the information structure – and then only from a technical perspective. Since an organisation consists of many interrelated information systems, both automated and manual, the big picture is enormous. 'Seeing' the causal effects of changing the way one or two apparently unrelated activities are conducted, requires quantum leaps of lateral association and a good knowledge of the overall process.

The conceptual distance between what is changed and the outcome of it can be enormous, so great in fact that it is analogous to being able to see beyond the horizon and around the curvature of the earth. It should therefore be no surprise that many significant information systems have been the result of intuitiveness rather than analysis. In this respect IT is teaching organisations some harsh lessons about themselves. Most organisations tend to understand themselves by the processes and procedures that go on within them. Few, however, understand how changing or extending the use of information can facilitate significant change within internal processes or open up new commercial opportunities.

The message now should be loud and clear, that exploiting information for commercial advantage is VERY difficult. Because, to all intents and purposes, you have to find something that was not there before. Not only does it require a sound knowledge of the processes within an organisation, the effect they have on each other and the significance of the information they generate; it also requires a sound knowledge of the capabilities of IT (in all its derivative forms) and an intuitive feel for an opportunity. This is the real challenge which faces today's organisations, knowing their mathematics, their market, their systems and the capabilities of both existing and emerging technologies.

NEW ORGANISATIONAL CHALLENGES FOR THE IT DEPARTMENT

Too many organisations are poorly structured to take advantage of information technology. Even though their commitment to IT is clear their structure and organisational relationships seem to prevent and stifle opportunity. Even though an organisation may be working hard to deliver business systems that make a significant contribution, organisational logistics often pose the biggest barrier.

The impact of IT on an organisation's structure and approach to management has received much attention, and many of the issues have already been discussed in this chapter. What has received far less attention are the ramifications of new technology, particularly its widespread use throughout the organisation and subsequently on the IT department itself.

It is now the IT department's turn to adapt. Many of the rapid changes in information technology are causing some organisations to reconsider the traditional role of the information technology manager and the structure of his department. Systems which have been designed to empower end-user development and moves toward out-sourcing of the day-to-day operations of hardware and software are challenging the traditional domains of the IT department.

Currently, several organisations are going through a very fundamental reassessment of what their IT Department ought to be doing and if, indeed, it needs to exist as a separate entity at all. In the UK, for instance, a consumer goods manufacturer, replacing its mainframe system with powerful networked microcomputers, believes its IT function may soon cease to exist. It envisages that systems management tasks that are not incorporated into the new systems will be conducted by end-users as part of their normal daily duties.

This belief is echoed by Des Lee, IT Director of B & Q, the do-it-yourself warehouse chain. He believes that in the future there will be no IT department as such, merely a centre for IT excellence. The centre's role, he believes, will be to act as mentors to end-users embarking on their own developments.

Clearly, the inference is that the organisational challenges for the IT department are as significant as those for the organisation as a whole. Technology has penetrated further and further into organisations to such an extent that it contradicts the rationale for a separate IT function. The requirement is for skills integration rather than specialisation. The challenge will be to disperse those skills throughout the organisation whilst at the same time maintaining a coherent systems architecture.

A balance must be struck between the need to organise IT facilities effectively whilst at the same time integrating the skills of an application developer within the organisation's day-to-day activities. Organisations will have to adopt a total rethink regarding the structure of their IT departments and ask themselves one very fundamental question: 'How many of the functions currently undertaken by our IT department should be undertaken within the business unit?' If this sounds like devolution, it should not. Devolution of IT responsibility was an initiative taken by many large companies to vest IT responsibility in strategic business units. Whilst a sound idea this initiative resulted in the business units setting up their own IT departments. The compartmentalisation remained albeit with smaller compartments. In order to integrate IT fully into the business, organisations will have to take far more radical steps than they have considered in the past. In future the concept of an identifiable IT function may be invalid. IT departments may have to be completely broken up, divesting themselves completely of development and maintenance responsibilities.

ENDNOTE

The availability of IT to so many areas within an organisation has radically changed the uses to which information is put. Whilst some notable initiatives have demonstrated the potential of information technology, the concept of exploiting information commercially remains difficult for many managers to grasp. Information for many managers and CEOs is still a low-level issue concerned with budget versus actual reporting, statistics and accounting. The notion that computers can turn information into a competitive weapon, can enhance a manufacturer's profit and can identify niche markets is an awkward concept for them to deal with. IT has until recently been considered a cost centre, something you have to have to run the business. And whilst the need for strategies for IT have been well understood, in terms of providing a cohesive operational support facility, applying it to open up revenue-maximising opportunities remain an anathema to many organisations.

Press reports of the case studies that have been published over the years have sounded a warning bell in the boardrooms of many companies that IT has now taken on a far greater commercial significance. Despite that acceptance, re-engineering the initiatives of competitors has proved both difficult and disappointing for many organisations. Their structure, culture and general way of doing things present major impediments to both the conceptualisation of new initiatives and the implementation process. IT, though frequently regarded as a tool for support is across a distant boundary when it comes to understanding its' contribution to a business development strategy. The connection, though clearly demonstrable in retrospect, is not obvious at the outset.

Information and IT when combined may be powerful strategic tools, but as with so many new tools there are few who are skilled in its use. IT now has significantly changed its role from the number-crunching monolith in the back room to that of a potential strategic weapon. But as with any weapon, before it can be used, the owner must learn how to prime, aim and discharge it. Knowing that IT has the capability to deliver a competitive advantage, form the basis from which a new business strategy might emerge, or radically change business processes, is not good enough. The real challenge for today's management is not to understand the nature of the technology itself but to appreciate and be cognisant of the business linkages that it is capable of forging and how these may be forged.

4 Can Success be Learned?

Despite the many significant question-marks over the ability of information technology (IT) to deliver, we are greeted from time to time by the odd success story or two. These 'pearls' show how some companies do, in fact, get it right and demonstrate the significant performance improvements which can be gained through the success implementation of IT. However, one problem is that these success stories, though well-known and publicised, are few and far between. Whilst representing only a tiny percentage of the total IT expenditure incurred by industry and government, they continue to be held up as paragons of IT virtue. Although few and far between they provide valuable and powerful lessons on just how significant the contribution of IT can be. Yet, despite detailed analysis of the nature of their initiatives, similar initiatives have proved difficult both to emulate and to define.

But successes they were, whether by design or sheer fluke. Is there anything that can still be learned from these already extensively analysed projects? Detailed below are case studies from IT's Hall Of Fame, each of which contributed significantly to corporate success.

Benetton

The Benetton group is an Italian-based, major fashion retailer with a global network of franchised outlets. Their product 'ethos' is built around a limited range of designs but with a vast availability of eye-catching, co-ordinated colours. Colours, rather than design or textile innovation is Benetton's trademark as its slogan 'United Colours of Benetton' confirms.

One of the major risks to Benetton is that they may wrongly anticipate consumer taste and hence demand for a particular colour (as opposed to style). Over-commitment to one particular colour which is not well-received by the customers could result in a significant financial loss. On the other hand, under-producing makes for a more expensive manufacture, inappropriate stock levels and lost sales.

To ensure that production and stock levels are commensurate with consumer demand, Benetton have made an imaginative use of their point-of-sale terminals to gauge customer preference. When an item is sold, the colour as well as the style is recorded and subsequently transmitted to an analytical database for further processing. This information is then analysed to determine current consumer preferences and to predict future demand. By doing this, Benetton can align manufacturing operations in accordance with consumer preference. Hence, the right number of garments are in the right place, at the right time. Therefore significant savings are made by not over-producing unpopular lines, and sales are maximised by ensuring availability of the most popular lines.

Thomson Holidays

Thomson Holidays is the largest package-holiday tour-operator in the UK, which was exactly what they set out to be.

Thomson Holidays set out to capture the major market share, not by price or quality differentiation, but by a two-pronged attack of providing information and offering a competitive commission structure for travel agents – their primary sales outlets. The whole thrust, although supported by TV and press advertising campaigns, was to make their products attractive to travel agents by speeding up the booking process and having more attractive commission rates than other tour operators.

By offering a higher commission, Thomson Holidays were immediately more attractive than their competitors. However, a quick defensive response from their competitors could be anticipated and any competitive advantage obtained from this single initiative would have been swiftly eroded. The second weapon in the Thomson armoury was the installation of terminals in travel agents' offices which were connected to the Thomson Holidays computer centre. Via these terminals, agents could check holiday availability and make real-time bookings. Not only did this allow travel agents to offer a superior service to those customers who chose a Thomson holiday, but paperwork was also reduced.

The two-pronged initiative of a competitive commission structure and a value-added service reaped the perceived rewards. Within twelve months, Thomson Holidays had achieved dominance in the packaged holiday market.

American Airlines

The American Airlines' case is somewhat similar to the above and further emphasises the significant advantage that may be gained by the provision of value-added services.

American Airlines' SABRE system allowed travel agents to book flight reservations for all airlines via a terminal sited in the agent's office. Whilst all airlines' flights were shown, American Airlines' flights to any particular destination were always displayed first – thus ensuring that their flights were always filled first.

As with the Thomson Holidays example above, there was a payoff for the agents using the system in terms of customer-service enhancement and a reduction in associated paperwork. The system was well-received by travel agents and soon 35 per cent of the American nation's travel agents were connected to SABRE. The effect of this system on the US airline industry was so profound (and painful to other operators in the market) that many airlines began to call 'foul'. In fact. Braniff Airlines blamed SABRE for their bankruptcy.

The SABRE system forged a special relationship between American Airlines and the travel agents by making travel agents' operations more effective and profitable. At the same time American Airlines was made the largest and most profitable airline in the USA. So significant was the contribution of SABRE that Bob Crandall, CEO of American Airlines has been quoted as saying he would sell his aircraft before selling SABRE.

In fact, American Airlines did sell SABRE, or rather 50 per cent of it, to a group of other US airlines for $650 million. Thus, even after achieving market dominance, the sale of 50 per cent share in SABRE must have recouped a significant proportion of the original development cost.

The SABRE initiative must be one of the finest examples of using IT to secure competitive advantage (if the Braniff contentions are true – SABRE could be considered as having actually *removed* some of the competition!). Since the introduction of SABRE many have tried to emulate its success but few have realised even a fraction of the return.

Caterpillar Tractor Inc.

Caterpillar Tractor Inc., is the largest US manufacturer of earth-moving, road-building and agricultural equipment. Spares and parts for maintenance and repair are stored and delivered worldwide from their Morton Parts Facility. However, spares were also stored at other Caterpillar sites and dealerships. This random distribution of spare parts often meant that customers were told that a particular component was out of stock when in fact it was available at another location. During the late 1970s, Caterpillar's management initiated a project to instal an on-line network to link these parts facilities together in order to provide a more responsive service for spare parts orders. However, on the back of the information now available, an idea for a new service was born. By virtue of the on-line network the company now knew the location and availability of all spares, and it was perceived possible to offer an express delivery (less than twenty-four hours) of spare parts to any location in the world. Even if the parts were not available at Morton they could be shipped from a field location nearest to the source of the order.

Caterpillar management, understanding the constraints placed upon construction contractors reckoned that they would be prepared to pay a premium price for such a service; if vital equipment broke down it would not need to lie idle for days, holding up work while the contractors waited for the spares to arrive. Their perceptions were correct as from the contractors' point of view the premium price paid for the spares was insignificant compared with the lost time on the job that might otherwise have been incurred. Caterpillar were so confident of their guaranteed twenty-four-hour delivery that they adopted a policy of 'No Charge' if the twenty-four-hour timeframe was exceeded.

The existence of this facility helped Caterpillar to gain a significant advantage over its competitors and to maintain its market share. Contractors chose Caterpillar on the basis, not of price, but of reliability and quality of service.

However, the benefits of the on-line network did not stop there. Because of the information that was now available to Caterpillar, it was realised that they could manage inventory on a national and, indeed, a global basis. By examining total inventory figures Caterpillar were able to reduce stocks of large and expensive parts knowing that, if required, they could be delivered from either Morton or another location. Their new system, crossing geographical boundaries, made it possible to manage total rather than local inventory levels. Obviously, benefits accrued from significantly decreased capital requirements for stock.

Caterpillar Tractor Inc., is one of the most interesting of the case studies as not only did the IT project fulfil its business expectations, but further, unexpected benefits accrued. It is a classic case of value being derived by unlocking previously unmanaged information.

Wells Fargo & Company

In 1983, Wells Fargo and Company, a prominent California bank, was a financial institution trying to be all things to every man. The bank was engaged both nationally and internationally in almost every aspect of retail and commercial banking.

On joining the Bank in 1983, its Chairman, Carl Reichardt, formulated a strategy which focused exclusively on regional retail financial services. The Bank's international business was curtailed and an IT strategy was put in place to support the transition to retail financial services and its ongoing operation.

Pivotal to the IT strategy was the customer information file (CIF) project. The CIF data, used in conjunction with demographic and economic information was used to determine geographic customer profiles and analyse the characteristics of customer/bank relationships therein. The system was originally devised to allow Wells Fargo Bank to know its customers better and to provide account executives with up-to-date customer-status information. Some time later, however, analysis of this information led to the identification of no fewer than 185 demographic regions within the state of California, each with its own profile of financial service requirements.

Because market characteristics had been defined in such detail, Wells Fargo was able to develop a portfolio of financial services products focused on the requirements of the specific subregion. Subsequently, this allowed each branch manager to determine which products to offer, based on the needs of his/her region. The effect of this initiative was to increase significantly individual branch performance and hence improved performance of the bank as a whole.

In this particular instance, whilst IT was not being employed to offer services, it was central to determining the marketing and product mix of each Wells Fargo branch. The benefits to Wells Fargo came from the identification of market segments which allowed them to focus their products more accurately on underlying customer requirements.

An Infallible Recipe for Success?

The foregoing case studies all show how some companies have invested successfully in IT and have achieved, in one way or another, a significant return on that investment. Can we learn anything further from these situations which may not have been considered previously. Do any of the case studies contain a secret formula, or even heuristic, which, if applied, can ensure successful IT investment?

These case studies are drawn from companies from many different sectors, such as engineering, travel, manufacturing and financial services. Their application of IT is just as varied: with the exception perhaps, of Thomson Holidays and American Airlines, their application of IT was as different as their industry sectors. So, whilst no similarities exist, we can at least draw some comfort from the following. It would appear that:

- No one type of company or industry appears particularly conducive to the application of IT to improve its performance.
- No particular usage of IT appears better than another for improving corporate performance.
- No particular type of technology or equipment appears dominant.

In order to identify the common threads which run through all the previous case studies, a broader perspective is required. If the specifics of the IT applications are disregarded for a moment two common attributes are evident in each and every case study:

- Most were an opportunistic response to a change in the business environment.
- The IT involvement is almost inseparable from the business initiative. In other words, IT was not an end in itself, it was an enabling influence – a servant of the business strategy.

ALL THAT GLITTERS IS NOT GOLD

None of these case studies are new, neither are my accounts of them as detailed as some earlier accounts of them. What I am about to explain in this section though is relatively new and has not previously been widely publicised. One of the major similarities shared between all the case studies is that none of the systems were new – all had been in operation for some time when new uses for them were identified.

For instance, with the American Airlines' SABRE system there is far more to the story than meets the eye, for it was originally conceived in 1959 (before its chief protagonists, CEO Bob Crandall and CIO Max Hopper joined the company). The original intention was to establish a centralised system for booking reservations made by the airline's ticket offices and travel agents. The issue of gaining a commercial advantage over their competitors was not at that time considered – and certainly not as any justification for proceeding with the development.

Changes within the market and the regulatory environment gave American Airlines their opportunity. The first of these was a series of failed attempts by the major airline operators and travel agents to establish a nationwide reservations system. American Airlines decided to go their own way and began marketing their system to travel agents. During the later deregulation of the US airline industry, SABRE was seen as a potential vehicle for promoting brand loyalty. By logging the number of times a customer flew with American Airlines and how far, the customer could be rewarded in some way with a retrospective volume discount. Thus the American Advantage Frequent Fliers programme was born. What happened afterwards is history and has already been well-documented.

Turning now to the Caterpillar Tractor and the Benetton examples, there, too, is much more than at first meets the eye. Benetton's manufacturing and inventory processes were already in place years before IT was introduced into the equation. True, IT speeded up the process and may have provided more accurate figures. But the underlying truth is that these operating principles, the brainchildren of Luciano Benetton, were already in place and IT, though important, was merely an extension of this operating strategy. Caterpillar Tractor's system was never conceived as a vehicle for providing a premium spare-parts delivery service. It was introduced as a means to locate inventory. It was only after the system had been installed that its potential to support a highly responsive customer service was seen.

By innovative thinking, *new* linkages between IT and the business were found. Caterpillar Tractor and Wells Fargo Bank identified new segments within their existing markets, Benetton saw a way to align their manufacturing output with consumer demand and American Airlines made themselves easier to deal with by providing new, attractive services. All these companies had one thing in common – breadth of strategic thinking. Information and IT were recognised as a potential strategic resource. This was not achieved by merely ramping up the IT budget; it was done by conceiving a potential contribution from IT to the key factors for success in their industry. And only when this had been determined did investment in new systems occur.

The key principle to accept is that information systems which make a significant strategic impact are not revolutionary, they tend to be evolutionary. They are not normally new systems but extensions (of either use or function) of existing systems. Nor are they the result of linear, analytical thought processes; they are opportunistic leaps of association. Furthermore, they are every bit as entrepreneurial as a bold new business concept. Markets were re-segmented, services differentiated and competitive positions were transformed. Most of all, these case studies attest to entrepreneurial ability applied to the capabilities of information systems.

Over the years there has been too much hype over strategic information systems. Far too much attention has been directed at the outcome of them, rather than their conception. IT can be strategic as it possesses the capability to transform, rearrange and reorganise information and associated processing activities. It is harnessing this capability, rather than copying the activities of others, that will allow a firm to become innovative with IT. To do this it is not good enough to rely on the activities of others to show the way. In order to manage the exploitation of information systems it is necessary to understand precisely what is to be managed.

Drucker, in *Managing in Turbulent Times,* cites the productivity of capital employed in an institution as the major factor in making a company outstanding. He gives several examples of companies (such as GEC, Siemens and British General Electric) who achieved superior results by achieving greater productivity of their capital employed. Clearly, you cannot have 'better' capital than someone else. You may have more or less, but ultimately one company's capital is much the same as that of another, only the quantity differs. The difference, according to Drucker, is the effectiveness with which the capital resource is managed.

The case studies which we have just reviewed are both the corollary and a microcosm of the broader concept put forward by Drucker. Neither their technology nor their information appears superior – nor, indeed, could have been. Why should Benetton's information have been better than that of their competitors? Considering that they are in the same business, they must have been generating similar information. Benetton, and the other examples in the case studies, succeeded in managing that resource far more effectively than their competitors – and consequently gained an 'edge'. Our case studies have shown that the companies mentioned achieved superior results by managing their information resource (available technology plus available information) more effectively than their competitors. This was achieved not necessarily by spending more on IT than their competitors but by directing attention towards information and activities that were key to their business.

5 Strategy

The issue of aligning IT to strategic corporate objectives has figured highly among the IT manager's list of concerns over recent years. Why this should be so may seem perplexing to the casual observer and begs the question 'Don't people talk to each other?' Can the issue be so simple as to require only a face-to-face meeting around a table, or the adoption of a rigorous, structured procedure? Or might there be a more subtle issue underlying the obvious symptoms?

A recent paper written by David Butler (formerly Chairman of the Butler Cox Foundation) identified the problems of a differing culture between the board of directors of a major company and its IT manager. In this paper, he relates a conversation he was having with the IT manager in which he questioned the manager on various financial operating statistics of his employer, such as turnover, market share, etc. The manager did not know and to add to this hapless soul's embarrassment, at the moment of his confession of ignorance, the chief executive just happened to be passing by. Except for a pair of raised eyebrows, the chief executive continued on his way – but for the IT manager the damage was done. He had 'proved' conclusively that both he and his department were totally out of touch with the rest of the management team. As if to re-emphasise this point, at a recent conference of the IT managers of top European companies, Paul Strassman reeled off a number of issues that typically figure among the concerns of board directors. He then turned to his audience and asked how many felt qualified to deal with such issues. From almost one hundred people attending this conference, those who affirmed their abilities in this area could be counted on the fingers of one hand.

A sad indictment indeed, and surely this must be the cause of the problem. Or is it? Perhaps if Mr Strassman posed the following question to the boards of directors of those same companies, a clearer picture of the problem might have emerged:

> You all have several major IT investments in the course of development within your companies. Can any of you explain the expectation you have of these projects in terms of your key business performance indicators?

I am not in the business of making predictions, but I would guess that the number of positive responses would have been just as paltry as that of the previous straw poll. There is clearly an issue in terms of the understanding of the strategic contribution of information technology and furthermore, it would appear that there is a need to establish some strategic 'common ground' between the business and IT. What is needed is some way by which the concepts which underlie terminology such as ROCI, return on assets and market share, can make the transition between the visionary perspective of the corporate strategist and the deterministic world of the IT practitioner.

WHY BOTHER WITH IT STRATEGY?

Given the perennial difficulties associated with the strategic alignment of IT and business objectives, perhaps it might be just as well to leave well alone. Most companies accept the need for some level of IT to keep certain operations viable. So why not just accept that it is part and parcel of the cost of being in business, that it needs a bunch of eccentric technicians to keep it running – and leave them to their own devices while the rest of the company gets on with the real world? The problem with that approach is that IT is here to stay. The handful of companies that do get it right do so in spectacular style. In addition, government and trade body initiatives compel industry at large and specific industry sectors in particular into the strategic management of IT. To ignore these trends is to act like the proverbial ostrich, and will ultimately spell doom, or at least relegation to the lower echelons of business, for the companies which adopt such an approach.

With the ever-growing pervasiveness of IT many companies are facing a situation where no IT strategy means no (or at least an incomplete) business strategy. IT is now becoming a principal method of achieving organisational goals (obtaining information, disseminating information, delivering services and processing work). Since information technology is so often at the top of the solution list for so many organisational imperatives, a lack of strategic and tactical plans for IT can ultimately manifest itself as a lack of organisational direction.

Strategy also forms a basic management control over company direction and performance. Without strategy, the only alternative control that can be exercised at executive level is via financial budgets. But budgets only set targets related to supply – supply of capital. They do not set direction with respect to the firm's markets, products or customers and only at a very superficial level can they be used to determine added value. Without a clearly focused strategy or mission in place, the organisation will become like a ship without sails – unable to pick up the driving force of the wind in order to set its direction on a chosen course and towards an ultimate destination.

Not all companies may see the need for an IT strategy. The less the strategic importance of information, the less rigour needs to be applied towards IT strategy determination. Where information is not considered to be a strategic resource, and where information management is demonstrated not to have a significant impact on the organisation, then it may rely on judgement and intuition. However, only the smallest of companies in non-information-intensive environments will enjoy such a luxury. For even non-information-intensive companies, as they grow larger, will evolve an organisational infrastructure and consequently adopt functional specialisations along these lines. Then even they will require certain levels of information in order to manage and operate effectively. Where companies are service-orientated, information-processing plays a crucial role in both operational effectiveness and gaining/keeping market share, and the absence of IT may even preclude entry into certain markets. IT strategy will prove to be vital for most organisations but just how vital depends on the nature of the business and its size.

PROBLEMS WITH PLANNING IT STRATEGY

Many organisations experience difficulty in determining strategy. In 1986 a Butler Cox Foundation survey identified four major barriers encountered during the formulation of IT strategy:

- difficulty in identifying the starting-point
- strategy formulation is a complex process with little proceduralisation
- business strategies are often inexplicit
- business strategy does not always translate into IT terms.

My own observations of strategy formulation and implementation raise two other issues:

- Strategies, like information, are passive. You can define one but making it happen is difficult, particularly at the business systems level.
- Current methodologies, though highly deterministic and rigorous, are merely conceptual models. Most are based on the assumption that a large part of the organisation has nothing better to do than formulate strategy. They tend to forget that an organisation is in the business of trading and service provision rather than strategy formulation. Also, a number of the methodologies currently in use were developed at different stages of evolution in the IT industry and therefore focus on the particular issues of that time, many of which are no longer so prominent today.

Herein lies the flaw of many strategies, particularly those relating to IT. They tend to be formulated in isolation and in abstract technical terms. Consequently the organisation's

IT strategy focuses on what is to be purchased rather than what areas of the business are to be improved.

WHAT MAKES A SUCCESSFUL STRATEGY?

In 1987 Goold and Campbell of the Ashridge Management Centre, published the results of their research work into the strategic style of sixteen multinational corporations. The objective of this research was to determine whether there was a single 'right way' to formulate, implement and monitor business strategy. The results identified three main models of strategic style (although several identifiable derivatives were also noted). The main styles were those of financial control, strategic control and strategic planning. Whilst the overall detail of this research is not appropriate here, as we are trying to determine the optimum IT strategy, the results of the work are thought-provoking for anyone involved in strategy formulation and implementation.

According to Goold and Campbell, three main strategic models were identified. The major differences between each model were attributed to the role played and level of control exercised by central management over business direction, coordination between business units and degrees of rigour exercised over budgets. Approaches ranged from financial control to strategic planning, with strategic control somewhere between the two.

Financial control strategy. Operating units were virtually autonomous, answerable to central management in respect of financial performances only. Companies using this strategy were generally focused on short-term returns (over a period of two to three years) and the major strategic planning document was the budget itself.

Strategic planning. This is typified by highly detailed, highly integrated planning documents.

Strategic control. This is less concerned with short-term budgets but focuses more on non-financial measures such as market-share and gaining competitive advantage.

One might think that with such vast differences in the methods of strategic management one approach must be right and the others wrong.

The results of Goold and Campbell's work is surprising because, despite the stark differences of strategic style the existence of one universal 'right way' was not established. All strategic approaches, when effectively implemented, brought about the desired results and all companies involved in the study are considered above-average performers. What was established, however, was perhaps even more significant; though no one approach was found to be consistently superior to any other, common success criteria, independent of the specific model used, could be identified. Each company displayed specific traits which significantly expedited the implementation and realisation of their chosen strategy. The following were identified as those attributes having the most significant effect on the successful implementation of a chosen business strategy:

- understanding the business
- open communication and mutual respect
- energy and common purpose.

Understanding the Business

Knowing the core issues rather than perpetually tinkering at the margins is a prerequisite for adopting an effective course of action. An in-depth understanding of the business, the overall market-place and the primary forces of change allows business initiatives to be undertaken on the basis of substantive and quantifiable fact. This is not an issue of mountains of company rule-books or a plethora of plans and forecasts. Rather, it is related to the depth and breadth of business understanding, how the organisation works (at all levels) and why it works that way. In large companies divisional specialities may direct the focus of individuals towards different aspects of particular issues, but overall the commitment to delve into the business and reach a common consensus of priorities is essential.

Open Communication and Mutual Respect

Ideas, information and opinions shared openly and with respect reinforces the concepts of common purpose and democracy and the feelings of inclusion and involvement. The 'ivory tower' and 'not invented here' attitudes have no place where the primary issue is one of influencing the behaviour of several thousand individuals. Trust also plays its part and must be explicitly conferred rather than vaguely implied. Trust is the cornerstone of respect and both are the result of open communication. Both act as catalysts for the 'can do' attitude both in terms of self-confidence and confidence of reward.

Energy and Common Purpose

The sharing of common goals and purpose throughout all levels of an organisation ensures that a common focus is achieved. This issue was also identified by Peters and Waterman in their book, *In Search of Excellence*, where they wrote of shared values holding together a company's overall strategy. It is interesting to note how all somehow locked together in some form of self-perpetuating system. Energy and common purpose can only come from open communication of corporate values and imperatives, which subsequently require trust on behalf of both management and workers – to be trusted to get the job done and trust in receiving fair reward for a job well done.

If there is no one right way to formulate a corporate business strategy then surely it is reasonable to suspect there is no one right way to formulate an IT strategy. As IT increasingly becomes part of the business itself, we should be focusing our attention not on the pursuit of a particular methodology but rather to plan our business while simultaneously determining those areas in which IT can make the most valuable contribution.

PERSPECTIVES ON CONVENTIONAL IT STRATEGY MODELS

As implementations of IT have grown in both the public and private sectors, so there has been an increasing awareness of the need for long-term planning of IT facilities and capabilities. Many strategy models and methods have been defined over the years and each has attempted to provide a framework for identifying 'a long view' with respect to the role of IT in supporting the particular business. Many have now fallen into disuse, either because they were not good approaches in the first place or because the usage of IT has changed to such an extent that the earlier methodologies no longer focus on the major issues.

But what is the right method? Or, in fact, is there one right method? For the purpose of this chapter, we should perhaps be looking for a strategic IT approach that best links into the corporate strategic model. But we have already established that there are several different types of business strategy model and none of these has been conclusively proven to be the 'right way'. Rather, they appear to be suited to particular types of company and perhaps to particular situations. Given that no one business strategy model is right for all organisations at all times, surely it must be reasonable to expect that no one IT strategic planning model will be right for all situations. It is more likely that from the base of current thinking on IT strategy, and the more enduring approaches that have survived, each may provide a useful perspective which might then enable some linkage with the business strategy.

IBM's Business Systems Planning (BSP)

Because of IBM's dominance of the IT industry and its influence over organisations using their equipment, BSP has been a dominant methodology for formulating IT strategy. It is strongly promoted by IBM in publications such as *The Information Systems Planning Guide* and by formal training courses held at a number of IBM locations worldwide. BSP has also inspired several derivatives, such as Honeywell's Planning Method and James Martin's Information Engineering.

The principal objective of BSP is to provide a mechanism for linking organisational strategy to an information systems plan, which would appear to be exactly what we are looking for. The BSP approach is to derive an information systems strategy by inferring management information and application systems requirements from elements of the organisation's business strategy. Though not specifically stated, the whole process pivots upon the assumption that business strategy is stated in a manner which would support the determination of tangible Management Information Systems (MIS) application objectives. A further important assumption is that the 'information analyst' who is responsible for identifying the applications is fully conversant with the business in question – that is, an expert in the business as well as systems, which is a very tall order indeed. If the latter attribute is not present within the information analyst, then it is highly likely that opportunities will be missed. At this highly formative stage, the risk of subtle divergences from the business objectives is high as the information analyst, by virtue of his training, will seek to determine what is currently being done rather than to project information systems into a strategic perspective. Even though the initial divergence may be slight, a difference in perspective is introduced and as more detailed analysis is conducted to form application specifications, the resulting information – systems perspective could be radically different from the business perspective.

But perhaps the biggest failing of BSP and potentially the cause of a major divergence in strategic business objectives is the fact that this approach specifically excludes some issues from the original analysis. BSP excludes from any strategic systems study issues over which the business 'has little or no control', which are defined as:

- economic
- government regulations
- market structure, defined as consumerism
- competition
- industry position/trends
- suppliers
- technology

Those familiar with business strategy planning will be aware that this could be a list of those issues which form the most significant strategic stimulae for most organisations and market sectors. Whilst individual businesses do not have the ability to influence any of these issues, they must certainly respond to them both tactically and strategically. Therefore, if the systems strategy method seeks to define applications at the strategic level, ignoring those factors which influence the business most, it is highly unlikely to provide any convergence with business strategy. In order for systems strategy and business strategy to stand any chance of alignment, they must share a common perspective from the outset. BSP does not appear to provide this and would seem almost to discourage it.

Critical Success Factors (CSF)

CSFs were used as a tool for setting organisational strategy long before information systems strategy became a corporate issue. CSFs are relevant to all types of business, small or large, high or low tech, and are defined as 'the limited number of areas in which, if they are satisfactory, will ensure successful competitive performance for the organisation. They are the few key areas where things must go right for the business to fluorish.' In banking, this might include gross margin, nett margin and cost/income ratios.

CSFs provide an extremely powerful focus on the major issues related to the business and can subsequently assist senior management in defining their information requirements. This can certainly prevent the occurrence of information overload and help to ensure that management receive only the information they require to control and direct the company. However, whilst CSFs may define the executive officer's information needs and assist senior management to monitor progress towards strategic goals, they do not provide any alignment between business and systems strategy. CSFs are concerned only with monitoring information related to strategy implementation, not with providing techniques for identifying applications which themselves support implementation of a chosen business strategy. Therefore, while CSFs provide a crucial input into determining the information requirements of strategic applications, they are not particularly useful in determining what those applications should be.

Nolan's Stage Methodology

Nolan formulated his stage methodology in the early 1970s whilst a lecturer at Harvard Business school and subsequently refined it during the ten years after he left Harvard to form his own consultancy. The methodology defines stages in the development of an organisation's IT infrastructure and subsequently seeks to project the organisation's future use of IT into the next stage by identifying a series of 'application opportunities'. A number of stages of IT evolution are defined by the methodology.

1. initiation (acquisition of computers)
2. contagion (period of intense applications development)
3. control (initiatives to control development and operations)
4. integration (service orientation, user support)
5. data administration (transition from technical management to information resource management)
6. maturity

Using benchmarks to establish the degree of technology involved in information-processing, IT-organisation characteristics, user-awareness, planning and control systems and the organisation's 'application portfolio', the firm's 'position' on the above scale is determined. Having established this the planner can then identify the required initiatives to make the transition to the next 'stage'. The method uses some highly subjective approaches such as the definition of a 'normative application portfolio' by considering 'the business functions that would be receiving DP support if the company had reached stage six – maturity'. The method also makes use of a ten-point plan to compare the current support for a given function and comparing it with that which 'should be provided'. Nolan then provides investment benchmarks to compare previous assessments in order to determine the required level of investment.

Nolan's method demonstrates a number of significant shortfalls in respect of aligning the information-system planning activities to the overall strategic direction of the company. First, it is highly orientated to determining the 'right' level of IT expenditure. The mere fact that a company may be spending less on IT than its competitors is not a problem in itself. Many companies have wasted small fortunes buying in IT-capabilities on the basis that their competitors were doing so rather than having any tangible expectation of the value such an investment might bring. It is more important to know that money is being invested in the right thing than to know how much is being spent overall. Furthermore the approach 'internalises' the strategic perspective on IT and uses as its foundation a highly conceptual model that has only the vaguest relationship with the business. Finally, the stage methodology falls into the same trap as BSP in that it ignores the strategic business stimuli which tend to drive the organisational strategy and hence its likelihood of converging with business imperatives is low.

The Nolan stage methodology is likely to create a situation whereby the IT functions of an organisation are insular and are potentially unresponsive to requests from business units. The stage methodology places undue emphasis on meeting certain (and highly subjective) investment targets for IT and the establishment of a predicated IT environment for the organisation in question. The approach may have some merit in determining a company's standing in terms of average IT-usage within a sector and may provide some information by which to conduct competitor analysis.

However, as an approach to calibrating business and IT strategy it is too prescriptive and parochial in its outlook.

Value Chain Analysis

The concept of 'value chain analysis' was originally put forward by Harvard Professor Michael Porter in his books *Competitive Strategy* and *Competitive Advantage.* His basic argument was that raw materials are turned into finished product by a series of internal processes (i.e. manufacturing, marketing, distribution, service) which he generically labels the 'value chain'. The processes within the value chain are those which 'add value' to the raw materials and consequently are the means by which any firm will gain a competitive advantage over others competing in the same market-place.

Porter then defines several ways in which a firm may add value (as perceived by its customers) to its products by refining its value chain. Five principal methods of competitive advantage are given:

1. differentiation;
2. cost;
3. innovation;
4. growth;
5. alliance.

Differentiation
This is the process whereby a company adds specific attributes to its products in order to make them identifiably different or superior in some way to those of its competitors. Differentiation is most commonly achieved by augmenting the product itself or by providing some kind of pre- or after-sales service.

Cost
Gaining competitive advantage via cost considerations centres on three concepts:

1. economies of scale;
2. cost advantage via scope;

3. cost advantage via information.

Economies of scale allow the acquisition, production, storage and distribution of products more effectively than competitors. If these savings are then passed on to the customer, the firm gains a cost advantage over its competitors whilst maintaining its required profit margins.

Cost advantage via scope refers to a firm's abilities to combine production costs of several products (throughout the value chain) or to undertake, in-house, certain processes that its competitors may be sourcing externally. As with the previous example, the advantage is gained by a lower cost to the consumer, whilst preserving previous margins.

Cost advantage via information is the means by which a company will turn its knowledge of a market – or specific processes within it – into lower production costs. It involves knowing the manner in which a competitor operates its advertising, credit or pricing policies; being in a position to match a competitor's promotional campaigns; understanding suppliers' pricing policies, or being able to compare simultaneously prices and conditions offered by a number of widespread, independent vendors.

The principle here is that possession of the information itself provides a capability to respond in the form of a more competitive pricing policy.

Innovation

This aspect of competitive strategy concerns the creation and adoption of new products or processes. It is an R&D driven issue which may result in the modification, rearrangement or development of new and enhanced products and/or processes. Product innovation is generally concerned with the development of new products or by augmenting existing products in such a way that product differentiation is achieved. Process innovation focuses on improvements in the production phase which may be translated into significantly increased quality (thereby supporting a strategy of differentiation) or significantly decreased costs (supporting economies of either scale or scope).

Growth

A growth strategy may be supported by either product or functional product growth. *Product growth* concerns the number of products a company may offer to its markets. *Functional growth* concerns the number of internally sourced functions (i.e. manufacturing, distribution) which a company undertakes in order to bring its products to the market. A growth strategy may be pursued as a supportive and precursive undertaking to product differentiation, cost reduction or innovation.

Alliance

Strategic alliances are formed to support the competitive strategy of one or more of the parties to the alliance. Broadly speaking, the purpose of the alliance will be to exploit the respective strengths of the parties to the alliance in order to obtain an advantage in one or more markets. Alliances may be forged by acquisition, joint venture or agreement.

With the ever-increasing importance of information and IT (and, it must be said, the considerable success of Porter's work) it is not surprising that there have been a large number of IT derivatives of Porter's framework. In fact, during 1987 there were over seventy methodologies around to instruct you on how to achieve competitive advantage via IT. Some focused on all the principles of competitive advantage while others concerned themselves with specific issues, such as differentiation.

However, despite the intensity of reporting, public seminars, books and case studies, within twelve months the situation had turned full circle. Chief executives began to question the value that IT was adding to their business. The sustainability of any competitive advantage achieved via IT was questioned and the overall contribution of IT fell under the microscope. Michael Porter's work was a significant insight into the general nature of 'adding value' and advanced our conceptual knowledge of how organisational processes may be exploited to provide industry leadership of one kind or another. Whether it and its IT-specific derivatives form the ultimate tool is as yet an unanswered question, yet the unarguable logic bolstered by fact make the concept a compelling choice.

What Michael Porter and his IT-orientated disciples provided were new perceptions, and they subsequently codified these perceptions into a formal, methodical model. Without new perceptions, learning never increases. Seeing what we have always seen from a different vantage-point opens up new opportunities. However, seeing and analysing are not doing, and having a method for doing the analysis will not implement anything. Despite the undoubted intelligence and logic contained in a methodology, possession of that methodology will not by itself instigate change. There is far more to the exploitation of information and information systems than merely method and analysis.

Customer Resource Lifecycle (CRLC)

In the December 1984 issue of *Communications of the ACM* (Association of Computer Manufacturers), Ives and Learmouth presented a customer-driven approach to IT strategy in their article 'Information Systems as a Competitive Weapon'. The central tenet of their thinking was that information is generated at various stages during a supplier/customer relationship and this relationship follows a generic cycle. This information, if exploited, could be used to gain competitive advantage over other firms in a similar market.

Their methodology is a thirteen-stage process and case studies are given to emphasise the use and value of the information gathered at each stage.

1. *Establishing Requirements*

Related to the decision to buy or replenish, companies can gain strategic leverage by providing easy access to information about their products. The initiative taken by Owens Corning Fiberglass to provide building companies with on-line access to evaluations of new insulation materials is an example of this.

2. *Specifying Requirements*
On receipt of a specific requirement a company can use IT to respond accurately and quickly. An example of this would be an inventory-locator service for airline spares which allows a quick and accurate response to a Request for Proposal (RFP) when they are received.

3. *Selecting Sources*
Using IT to locate the most appropriate service or product is particularly suitable for companies which act as intermediaries. Broking companies can use IT to locate goods and/or services for their customers quickly and efficiently. These locator services can provide comprehensive and wide-ranging searches which could not be supported by paper systems.

4. *Order*
IT can make the placing of an order easier and faster and can provide almost instantaneous confirmation. Airline reservation systems present a particularly good example of this.

5. *Authorise and Pay*
IT can make this process quicker, less error-prone and sometimes more secure. Obtaining authorities to spend, making electronic payments and credit-card authorisation systems are all examples of this.

6. *Acquire*
Using IT to deliver goods and services to a customer can confer a commercial advantage by making life more convenient for the customer or by giving greater flexibility in the availability of the service. Examples of this are automated teller machines (ATMs) open for twenty-four-hour use, purchased software downloaded to a PC (as provided by Telecom Corporation) and the downloading of economic data to PCs as provided by DRI Corporation.

The key issue here is of using IT to provide the product or service where and when your customer wants it.

7. *Test and Accept*
IT can be used to verify the acceptability of goods and services. Western Union have a system which matches freight-shippers with motor freight-carriers but also confirms that the carriers are authorised and properly insured to carry particular goods.

Another example, is the Medicare Glaser Company which provides a service to run a check on prescriptions against other drugs being taken by the customer to avoid interaction problems.

8. *Integrate into and Manage Inventory*
Providing information to customers regarding their own inventory is an approach adopted by Westraco, a paper supplier. They advise their customer's system when a shipment is made. On arrival a bar code on the shipment is then used to add the details to the customer's inventory, simultaneously confirming delivery.

9. *Monitor Use and Behaviour*
By using IT to analyse trends, a superior level of support may be provided to a company's distributors and agents. For instance, ARA Magazines monitor returns and then predict the number of magazines a retailer should take. This not only helps ARA to contain production costs but also prevents the retailer from purchasing unnecessary stock. Likewise, Fidelity Brokerage supports its agents by giving them access to their system to buy or sell stocks, maintain portfolios and track price movements of up to eighteen stocks.

10. *Upgrade if Needed*
Some companies use IT to upgrade their distributors' inventories automatically if changes in demand are perceived. For instance, a greetings-card supplier selects appropriate cards for its retailers according to market demands and upgrades their inventory as necessary.

11. *Maintain*

During their life, products may need repair or servicing and IT can be used to provide a superior service in this respect. One example of this is the use of PC systems by car dealers to predict when a service is due so that they can notify their customer.

12. *Transfer and/or Dispose*

When a customer has finished with a product or service, IT can be used to make the returning process easier and quicker. Avis, for example, use card-based ATMs to shorten the car-rental return-time and provide an automated receipt.

13. *Account For*

IT can be used to record and monitor expense on a particular service. One instance of this is the American Express Corporate Card which records all travel-related expenses and provides a detailed statement of all expenditure.

CRLC like many methodologies provides a useful, though far from complete, perspective on the potential applications of IT. Whilst it is true to say that without customers there is no business, IT can provide significant benefits elsewhere in the company. The Ives and Learmouth approach does not take this into account.

If CRLC is seen as a panacea (rather than one useful perspective) there is a danger of over-focus on this issue. This could potentially give rise to over-engineered solutions which, though technically feasible, may add no value to the core product. Whilst CRLC identifies many useful applications, it misses several issues which are generally accepted to increase customer satisfaction and generate loyalty. Product-related issues of quality, response to customer requests and reliability are not comprehensively addressed. Hence, CRLC is a product of its underlying case studies rather than a comprehensive approach to supporting customer service via information technology.

METHODOLOGY OR MYTHOLOGY

Is there a panacea for strategy formulation at either the business level, the IT level or both? I think not: the models which we have reviewed in previous sections have had their day – they belong to a different age, to more predictable times. The rigorous, deterministic approach to strategy formulation is no longer applicable to today's fast-moving, ever-changing business environment. And if this is true of the business environment then it naturally follows that the determination of supporting IT strategy will be just as difficult and elusive to pin down.

Historically, the production of formal strategy documents, broadly speaking, fulfils two major criteria:

1. it serves to communicate management's vision of the future;
2. at the more detailed levels it provides a means to prepare and calibrate the whole organisation in pursuance of the strategic vision.

The vision provided the target while the detailed plan ensured that all parts of the organisation were pointing in the right direction. In response to the detailed strategic business plan, Data Processing (DP) executives responded with proposals for large integrated operational and MIS systems. But as the pace of business accelerated and specialisation (serving specific niche markets) and internationalism increased, events overtook these large, relatively slow moving projects. But many of these methods still prevail in many major institutions – and are failing to keep pace with the ever-changing business environment. Yesterday's IT strategy models served us reasonably well – *yesterday* – but they rely on the business environment remaining predictable – which it is not. The issue we are facing is not one of aligning strategy; the issue is one of IT's capability to keep up with the pace of change – alignment does not even come into it. The major problem facing the major corporations of today is not their capability to produce a detailed strategic plan. It is that the business environment as a whole is anathema to such a process.

To formulate any corporate strategy to the degree of detail from which any subordinate strategy can be determined (be it IT, human resources, etc.), requires that one major assumption remains true throughout the strategic term: that of relative constancy. Whilst the whole concept of strategic planning attempts to predict the future and subsequently prepare for it, the underlying assumption is that tomorrow will be largely the same as today. In other words, strategy planning, whilst it attempts to introduce change, assumes that such change will be gradual and predictable. Given such a strategic plan, the extraction of an IT strategy was relatively straightforward and could be formulated in such terms as:

- Anticipation of vertical growth of markets and the organisation as a whole. Hence 'IT Strategy' could be expressed in terms of capacity, throughput and facility.
- Alignment of IT facilities with manufacturers' strategy to avoid obsolescence and incompatibility.

The whole process was fairly mechanistic and predictable. Today's business environment, however, is typified by increasing globalisation, markets continually fragmenting into smaller niches and the speed of introduction of new products. Nothing could be more at odds with these previous, predictable, times than today's volatile, changing environment. The only thing that can be predicted with some confidence is that significant change will occur at some time. This whole situation defies planning and prediction, and this prevents the application of rigorous structured planning models. What is required to survive in this environment is fluidity, not rigidity. It requires the existence of a responsive environment, not a regime that clings on to previously held assumptions.

Over the past few years, I have read many articles from various sources which address the issue of aligning IT strategy with business strategy. All, however, seem to miss two vital points. The first is that it is almost always assumed that a business strategy exists in the first place. This is not the case and many organisations, because of the situation outlined above, have abandoned detailed strategy formulation –

because they are generally superseded before the ink is dry. Consequently, the issue of aligning subordinate strategy is a complete 'red herring' because there is nothing to align it to. The second issue, however, is far more significant as it shifts the context of IT strategy away from the purely technical issues of capacity and throughput.

Previous IT strategies were predominantly concerned with the issues of performance and capacity. Business systems also tended to figure in these terms and as such were considered in the light of rewrites to take advantage of new hardware/software platforms, 'enlargements' to deal with anticipated volume increases and 'internal enhancements' (i.e. interfaces to other systems). Today's business environment has created a fundamental shift of emphasis away from this to a need for new or drastically enhanced business systems. In today's IT environment the requirement for capability is taking precedence over capacity.

As IT has played an ever-increasing role in an organisation's business operations, it has become increasingly sensitive to change in the business environment. And no matter how sophisticated the development tools that are available, people can change the way they do things quicker than a computer can be re-programmed. Business operations and the underlying automated systems have become so inextricably intertwined as to become inseparable. In such a situation, words such as 'alignment' and 'calibration' become irrelevant – business operations and the supporting applications are one and the same thing; they have become truly integrated. In addition, they belong not to the IT department – they belong to the user. It is the user who should determine the strategic perspective on his applications, not IT. IT can only deliver a development service; the business efficacy of any given business system is delivered by the users and it is the user's responsibility to ensure that this is the case.

Methodologies: Why Common Sense Does Not Work

Adopting a logical, step-wise process is an attractive proposition – particularly when such an approach is delivered to our desks. 'Just follow the easy-to-learn steps and we can grind the competition into the dust' may not be the words used, but is often the attitude. When organisations see their competitors developing new products or taking new initiatives, many executives begin to wonder 'What do they do that we don't?' Unfortunately they draw the wrong conclusion which is to believe that their company is light on the particular techniques that their competitors must be using.

Enter new methods, new techniques, new studies, new planning forms, new corporate buzz words and slogans. And that's it – little else changes. Techniques by themselves are nothing more than aspirin and sticking plasters for a deeper corporate malady. No matter how much common sense is inculcated within the technique, no matter how well-intentioned company management are, if the techniques do not become translated into guiding principles at all levels within the company, they will wither and die.

The reason is simple – in isolation strategic techniques are nothing more than words and diagrams on paper – they do not, of themselves change anything.

Quick Fixes and Magic Spells

Thus far we have reviewed several of the most prominent methodology models which aim to integrate IT into strategic thinking and action. This apart, all the offerings have several other characteristics in common: they have been compiled by eminent experts in their field and they contain a wealth of good old common sense. Takes Ives and Learmouth's CRLC, for example – if you wanted to use IT to create a superior customer service (and subsequently increase market share), does it not make sense to direct IT investment towards the information-related activities that you undertake for your customers? Of course it does. Or consider Michael Hammer's re-engineering; since IT overcomes the need for many of the controls required in paper systems, should not IT investment be directed towards making internal processes more effective? Of course, no one would argue with that.

There are literally hundreds of methods and techniques to establish how a company should be applying IT. Yet the issues of true integration between IT and corporate strategy continue to dominate the industry and remain elusive. The business community in general, and IT in particular, exists within a cacophony of technique.

There is not one aspect of IT, whether it is strategy formulation, systems design or operations management, but there always seems to be an all-encompassing technique available – at a price. Yet, despite this wealth of technique, the overwhelming message is one of companies who suffer from poor quality systems, expensive, inefficient data centres and systems which do not support business goals.

One Size Fits All?

Before considering what is presented in the following sections of this chapter, consider Table 5.1. On the vertical axis is a list of companies which have significantly improved their business by the innovative use of IT and the particular application that provided it. On the horizontal axis are the major attributes of the better known IT strategy models – some of which have already been discussed. Notice anything? Of course, one application example fits more than one model. Which demonstrates at least one thing – that there is no one right way to look at IT strategically and one person's perspective is not necessarily better than that of another.

Despite the many strategic 'flavours' that are presented by the methodologies we have reviewed, many of the case studies used to support and define these methodologies fit other methods equally well. This rams home one essential truth about the strategic direction of IT – that there is no one right way to do it. If we were to include some of the lesser-known models which have been based on specific aspects of Michael Porter's value chain, this fit would become even more generalised (however, space and the interests of brevity preclude this essentially repetitive exercise).

The reason for this generalised fit is the result of a common paradox – that two people can look at the same thing, perceive something quite different – and both be right! The problem associated with formulating an approach based purely on anecdotal material, no matter how much of that material is gathered, is that the significance of the attributes becomes somewhat personalised to the researcher. The majority of the methodologies today have been formulated in this manner, their particular components being derived from the attributes of the various case studies under analysis. There may be other attributes, equally significant, that were either not noticed or were disregarded.

To add weight to this argument, there are two common aspects which run through the majority of these case studies. However, they are related not to the outcome (i.e. the specific systems solution) but rather in the manner in which they were conceived. Two common traits remain consistent in the majority of cases:

1. None were conceived by the methods proposed by the methodologies which cite them as examples.
2. Few followed any 'conventional' process of strategic planning. They were the brainchild of one or more opportunist(s) within the company who saw the opportunity to improve the business in some way.

Studying the use of IT, whether it is to understand the capabilities of a particular technology or to determine specific applications within an industry (for instance, transport) or functional (for instance, marketing) sector is both a valid and a useful exercise. Exercises such as this are essential to conducting comparative analyses of a firm's system in relation to its competitors and emerging industry trends. Equally important is that such exercises foster a continual learning process in understanding the capabilities of IT. Analysing the outcome or results of a particular initiative of innovation will give no indication of how the transformation from concept to product was made possible.

A particularly good example is that of the American Hospital Supply Co. Their strategic information system allowed hospitals throughout the USA to submit orders directly through a VDU installed on their premises. This

Table 5.1 Strategic information systems

Case	*Country*	*Sector*	Value chain analysis: *Customer Resource Life-cycle*	*Re-engineering*	*Differentiation*	*Exploiting Niches*	*Influencing Costs*	*Looking in Trading Partners*	*Creating New Businesses*	*Changing Business Processes*	*Creating New Products/Services*	*Application*
Abbey Life	UK	Insurance	✓		✓			✓		✓		Portable micros as aids for sale presentations
ACCORD	UK	Retail	✓	✓		✓		✓				Forging manufacturer–distributor links through an ordering system
Aetna Life	USA	Insurance	✓		✓			✓				Customer access to insurance database
AGVO Opel	Germany	Car dealer	✓							✓		Sales support system with extensive customer information base
American Hospital Supply customers	USA	Medical products distribution		✓		✓			✓			On-site order entry by
Akzo	Netherlands	Chemicals and paints	✓		✓	✓		✓				Information systems for car 'body' shops
Alco Standard	USA	Paper	✓	✓	✓		✓					Speeding up inventory turnover using management system
American Air Lines	USA	Transport	✓		✓	✓		✓				On-line airline reservation system

American Express	USA/Worldwide	Finance services	√		√					√		Extensive systems for operations support and expansion
ARA	USA	Magazine distribution	√		√			√				Using IT to add value to distribution links
ARCO	USA	Oil		√			√		√	√		Price notification system
Bank of America	USA	Banking	√	√	√	√		√				Cash management for corporate customers
Bank of Scotland	UK	Banking	√	√		√			√		√	Home banking on videotex
Bank One	USA	Banking		√	√				√	√	√	Strategic development of electronic delivery systems
Beecham Foods	UK	Food					√					Private videotex used by sales staff in their homes
Benjamin Moore	USA	Paints		√	√			√		√		Using IT to analyse and match colour
Boeing Aircraft	USA	Aircraft		√						√		Electronic transmission of Computer Aided Design (CAD) information
British Home Stores	UK	Retail		√	√			√		√		Electronic data interchange for deliveries
Brooke Bond Oxo	UK	Food		√			√			√		A back-office voice-response system used by sales staff
CARDIS	USA	Freight bureau service		√			√			√		A cargo data-interchange system
Car/Puter	USA	Car broking bureau service	√		√		√			√		Detailed pricing information for car buyers
Cataline Marketing	USA	Service	√	√		√						Retail coupon targeting system
CCN	UK	Credit rating				√			√			A national on-line credit-checking service
Cigna Corporation	USA	Insurance	√	√		√		√	√	√		Corporate access to regional insurance files
Comp-U-Card	USA/(UK)	Service					√					Teleshopping through videotex
Courage Take Home Trade	UK	Drinks	√	√	√		√	√				Portable micros used by salesforce

Table 5.1 Strategic information systems (*contd*)

Case	*Country*	*Sector*	*Customer Resource Life-cycle*	*Re-engineering*	*Differentiation*	*Exploiting Niches*	*Influencing Costs*	*Looking in Trading Partners*	*Creating New Businesses*	*Changing Business Processes*	*Creating New Products/Services*	*Application*
			Value chain analysis									
Courtaulds	UK	Textiles					✓					The use of Value Added Network (VAN) service in ordering and distribution
Digital Equipment Corporation	USA/Worldwide	Computer manufacturer	✓	✓	✓					✓		Expert systems to configure customer specifications
Delta Airlines	USA	Transport		✓			✓					Strategic pricing using information technology
Distriphar	France	Pharmaceutical distribution	✓		✓		✓	✓				Videotex-based VAN service for ordering
Eastman Kodak	USA/Worldwide	Photographic			✓					✓		Personal computer-based system
Federal Express	USA	Courier	✓	✓								Facsimile-based document delivery service
First Boston Bank	USA	Finance (mortgages)		✓	✓			✓		✓		An electronic mortgage network
General Electric	USA	Household appliances	✓		✓					✓		Product database for better customer service

General Foods	USA	Food	√		√			√			Bar-coded data analysis for market research
General Tire	USA	Tyre manufacturer	√	√			√			√	Telemarketing as a customer service
Glaxo Pharmaceuticals	UK	Pharmaceuticals	√	√			√				Integrated IT for manufacturing and administration
Golden Wonder	UK	Food		√	√		√			√	Microcomputers in delivery vans
Hewlett Packard	USA	Computer manufacturer	√		√						A network linking manufacturers with suppliers
Hill Samuel	UK	Finance		√	√		√	√		√	Videotex for information dissemination in a large company
Holiday Inn	USA	Hotels	√			√			√		Video teleconferencing and entertainment for hotel guests
ICI	UK	Chemicals		√			√			√	Personal computers for mobile salesforce
Inland Steel	USA	Steel	√	√						√	Steel ordering and monitoring system
Intermodal Transportation	USA	Transport	√		√					√	Price-quoting system using networked microcomputers
John Deere	USA	Agricultural equipment		√	√		√	√			On-line database for component availability
Lederle Laboratories	USA	Pharmaceutical								√	Voice messaging for field staff
Karstadt	West Germany	Department store		√						√	IT as a multi-level retail tool
Louisiana Oil and Tire	USA	Oils and Tyres		√			√			√	Teleselling as a means of increasing sales volumes
Mannington Mills	USA	Textiles	√	√	√			√			The use of colour graphics as an information and sales tool
McDonnell-Douglas	USA	Aircraft		√						√	Computer-aided design with links to suppliers

Table 5.1 Strategic information systems (*contd*)

Case	*Country*	*Sector*	Value chain analysis: *Customer Resource Life-cycle*	*Re-engineering*	*Differentiation*	*Exploiting Niches*	*Influencing Costs*	*Looking in Trading Partners*	*Creating New Businesses*	*Changing Business Processes*	*Creating New Products/Services*	*Application*
McKesson	USA	Pharmaceutical	√		√							Electronic goods-ordering
MEMA	USA	Motor equipment		√			√	√		√		Data network for the automobile trade
Merrill Lynch	USA/ Worldwide	Finance	√		√		√		√			On-line cash management package
Milliken	USA	Design company	√		√							Computer-aided design system for carpets
Mobil France	France	Oil	√						√			A voice-messaging system for sales and marketing
Mothercare	UK	Retailing	√	√	√					√		Videodisc as a sales aid
Neckermann Versand	Germany	Mail Order		√	√			√		√		On-line ordering systems for mail-order company
Nexis	USA/Worldwide	Information Service				√			√			Electronic database
Norton	USA	Manufacturing	√		√					√		On-line ordering and pricing system for distributors

Owen Corning	USA	Glass	√		√	√		√			Information and sales database for the building trade
J.C. Penney	USA	Department store		√		√			√		Point-of-sales system for credit authorisation
Pitney Bowes	USA	Office equipment	√	√	√		√	√		√	Information technology to speed up customer service
Publix	USA	Supermarkets	√	√	√					√	The use of EFTPOS on an ATM infrastructure
Quelle	Germany	Mail order	√	√	√			√		√	Videotex and voice-response ordering system
Red Lion Inns	USA	Hotels	√		√			√			Setting discounts through a reservations network
Red Lobster	USA	Restaurants		√			√			√	Strategic pricing for nationwide restaurants
Red River Construction	USA	Construction		√			√				Pricing system for contract bidding
Schlumberger	France/USA	Oil equipment					√	√		√	An expert system for oil exploration
Sears Roebuck	USA	Department store	√			√				√	Direct mail marketing using a customer database
Security Pacific	USA	Banking	√	√	√	√		√	√	√	Credit-checking system for car dealers
SEEBoard	UK	Public utility	√	√	√					√	Products database on videotex in retail outlets
Shell	UK	Oil	√		√			√		√	Analysis of fuel purchases using portable data capture
Singer	USA	Electrical appliance retailer	√	√			√	√		√	A merchandise ordering system
Southlands Corporation	USA	Foods		√			√			√	Using a computer network to eliminate in-store inventory
State Farm	USA	Insurance	√		√					√	Electronic policy system for agents

Table 5.1 Strategic information systems (*contd*)

Case	*Country*	*Sector*	*Customer Resource Life-cycle*	*Re-engineering*	*Differentiation*	*Exploiting Niches*	*Influencing Costs*	*Looking in Trading Partners*	*Creating New Businesses*	*Changing Business Processes*	*Creating New Products/Services*	*Application*
			Value chain analysis									
Supervalu	USA	Supermarkets		√			√	√		√		Electronic data interchange in the food industry
Telcot	USA	Cotton		√		√				√		Electronic cotton trading system
Telspar	UK	Supermarkets		√			√	√		√		A value-added order-entry system linking wholesaler and retailer
Thomson Holidays	UK	Travel	√	√	√			√			√	Videotex-based travel reservation system
Ticketron	USA	Entertainment	√	√	√	√		√		√		A network supplying an entertainment booking service
USAA	USA	Automobile insurance			√			√		√		Sales and automated records
USA Today	USA	Newspaper		√	√		√			√		Electronic newspaper transmission
Verenigde Bloemionveiling	Netherlands	Cooperative		√			√			√		The use of IT in flower auctions
Vestric	UK	Pharmaceutical distributors	√	√	√		√	√		√		Electronic ordering from retail premises

Wall Street Journal	USA	Newspaper		✓	✓	✓		✓	Global transmission of newspaper
Westinghouse Electric	USA	Electrical	✓	✓	✓		✓	✓	Customer terminals for order entry

Source: Reproduced with permission of CSC INDEX.

conferred several advantages on the user, such as reduced processing-time for orders and quicker turnaround of supplies. However, the most interesting aspect of this system was not its outcome (significant though this was for AHS) but how it actually came into being:

While waiting for an appointment, an AHS salesman observed a clerk inputting orders to the hospital computer, to be ultimately dispatched to their suppliers. He then considered the potential benefit to both the hospital and AHS if the clerk could have input those orders directly to the AHS computer system. After his ideas had been discussed with colleagues, development began on one of the most strategically significant initiatives in the US medical supplies market.

Now, this salesman did not have a methodology tucked under his arm! Just what did spark off this association between a business service and his perception of how IT might support it? The two major issues which have to be considered in this and most 'breakthrough' applications are these:

1. They are conceived not as a result of prescriptive procedure but emerge as a result of lateral thinking. The outcome is 'technology transfer', a situation where lateral thinking links together a conceptual business initiative with IT as a potential solution to, and enabler of, the initiative.
2. The culture within AHS allowed the idea to blossom into a full-blown business system. An idea coming from the front line of the business was quickly 'bought into' and acted upon by the senior management of AHS.

I am persuaded that the ultimate differentiator between the average systems solution and those that significantly add value to a company has nothing to do with the methods and procedures that are in place. It has far more to do with the *quality of thinking* within the organisation and an organisational structure and philosophy which is conducive to turning ideas into initiatives and, ultimately, solutions.

By way of further confirmation of the above, the reader is again referred to Table 5.1 and in particular the first column.

The companies quoted have more than just their innovative use of IT in common. They are also leading companies in their field and their pre-eminence is widely attributed to their management philosophies and attitudes towards fostering innovation and encouraging initiative. Excellent management, it appears, rubs off on the way you use IT.

Of course, this should come as no surprise. Information is present within everything we do in corporate life. It must therefore follow that for a resource with so many uses and as many potential solutions, prescriptive procedures can neither cover nor anticipate all eventualities. Strategic systems (and they may be large or small, highly visible to the customer, or internal) emerge not as a result of process. They emerge by one or more informed individuals within the organisation seeing the potential of IT to support or contribute to the organisation's overall mission. Such systems may be:

- totally new;
- existing systems for which new uses are seen;
- existing systems which may be extended to provide new facilities.

What the systems are and what they turn out to be is largely unimportant. The nut to crack is to understand how IT innovation occurs, who does it and how to harness that resource.

Whoops – We Thought We'd Got It Right!

What the previous section has shown is that there is no one, universal, way to think about IT and subsequently direct investment. It would appear that, regardless of their particular emphasis, most of the recognised 'right ways' fit several situations. And, just to rub salt into the wounds, none of those strategically significant systems resulted from any of the analytical processes prescribed by the 'right' methodologies.

The issue is, of course, one of interpretation. All the popular methodologies have come out of academic studies of the case studies similar to those summarised in Table 5.1.

Therefore, the major attributes of the case studies have been those which at first seemed important to the researcher. These attributes have subsequently been expanded into a methodology by the researcher. Now this is not meant as an attack on those individuals – their work has been invaluable in providing us with a 'lens' by which to view IT from a particular corporate perspective. The problems arise when they are treated as a holy grail, for they are in fact only one way of looking at the issue.

Searching for holy grails is a particularly human trait, related, perhaps, to our innate inquisitiveness. In business, however, they tend to become fads as each map to the elusive holy grail quickly becomes superseded by another. The danger of seizing one particular solution to the exclusion of all others can be well-illustrated by a frantic search for a holy grail which occurred some 300 years ago.

In Europe during the mid-1600s, the inhabitants of the major cities, and London in particular, were suffering from a terrible and widespread disease; the bubonic plague. The mortality rate from the disease affected a huge proportion of the population – to the extent that in London there was a real fear that the capital may have to be abandoned.

Not surprisingly, many experts appeared on the scene with many methods to prevent the city-dwellers contracting the disease. Most of these cures were formulated by studying the healthy, rather than the sick. Consequently, depending on which healthy group of people were studied, various 'black death avoidance strategies' were spawned, for example:

- People who only drink wine do not catch the plague.
- People who only drink water do not catch the plague.
- Atheists are not infected.
- Catholics do not get infected.

With the scientific knowledge available to us today the above notions would be rejected as ridiculous. However, with the level of knowledge around in those days, there was never a shortage of people ready to line up behind one creed or another in order to avoid infection. The breakthrough in conquering the plague came only when painstaking research identified the source of infection and the manner in which it occurred.

Many of the above criticisms can be applied within the method-hungry business community. The majority of the methodologies reviewed here (particularly the more recent ones) have been formulated by analysing the results of IT innovation rather than concerning themselves with how it occurred in the first place.

It is my experience that there is something more than mere method and technique involved in IT innovation. By analysing the outcome of the various case studies we can learn useful perspectives. However, there are deeper issues to be addressed if a company wishes to compete and emulate rather than simply copy and follow – striving to be second best is a dangerous strategy.

I am unaware of any consultancy or business school which can make the claim that their techniques succeed where all others fail. Whilst leading companies are analysed *ad infinitum* to discover their secret, none of the proceduralised approaches which emerge from these exercises prove to be the holy grail of the ultimate solution. I believe there are two main reasons for this:

- What makes a company 'tick' and drive it constantly toward renewal is more than procedures. It is a blend of control, quality and initiative. And whilst control and quality systems can be prescribed and continually refined according to industry sector, initiative cannot. The desire and confidence to take initiative, to perceive a strategic IT opportunity is essentially a cultural issue which is rooted more in principles and beliefs rather than systematic process.

In essence, purely adopting a process for analysing, planning or implementing systems will not result in a 'switched on' company.

- Most IT strategy models assume that the business strategy is both known at all levels and that the detailed tactics of execution are known at the time when the IT strategy starts. This in my experience has hardly ever been the case and in any event does not take into account one major issue; that the tactical plan that looks good now may be completely superseded in three years' time. Even though the strategic goal may hold firm, the tactical path for getting there may alter radically as time and circumstances change.

Information is a critical resource but requires new and radical organisational structures to exploit and direct it. The companies featured in Table 5.1 have not just recognised this, they have 'bought into' the concept and organised it. It is no coincidence that so many of the leading innovators in IT are themselves recognised as leading companies *per se.* Those very philosophies that make them leading companies percolate through the organisation so that as a result, their IT initiatives also have the leading edge.

HOW AN IT STRATEGY HAPPENS

Very few IT strategies arrive formally, they tend to emerge as smaller projects prove their worth and demonstrate wider capabilities. This is particularly true when new technologies are involved. Rigorous, longer-term plans emerge as a requirement to control and direct small 'start' systems which have been seen to have wider organisational applications. In this instance 'strategy' is a charter for IT-driven organisational change.

Having a detailed strategic plan from the outset and at any particular time satisfies a psychological rather than a corporate need. Since time immemorial, man has striven to predict the future. Detailed plans which attempt to ordain the events that will occur over a period of years are more related to satisfying this need than to the process of effective change management. It is as if there were a philosophy that states 'if we write down what we want the future to be, then it will occur'.

The grandiose schemes which propose the total redevelopment of many or all applications and their supporting infrastructure are generally doomed from the start. The bigger the endeavour, the longer the lead time to implementation, then the greater the number of assumptions there will be in the plans. The words of Charles Handy provide a memorable lesson:

> The multiplicity of variables impinging on any one organisational situation is such that data on all of them sufficient to predict the outcome of that multiple interrelationship would never, in practice, be forthcoming... (Charles Handy, *Understanding Organisations*)

When a company attempts to implement an all-encompassing IT strategy, several 'trip wires' thwart their efforts:

- You cannot legislate for creative thinking to occur at a particular point in time. A significant opportunity may occur several months after a direction has been set and resources allocated.
- Changing the technical infrastructure tends to spin off many smaller projects as the full ramifications become clear. Projects to manage/define interfaces determine interim solutions until 'the next release' is available. Security, performance, contingency, training, recruitment, etc., all occur as the full significance of the changes become understood. This all contributes to a situation of project drift, where the observable relevance of any one project to the overall mission becomes increasingly less discernible.
- Many of the assumptions regarding capability only become apparent at late stages in a project. To a large, expensive project which is critical to the business these last-minute revelations can give rise to significant con-

cern. Not only does the realisation of perceived benefits become questionable, but reputations are on the line. Consequently, expediency and politics become the dominating issue and both the functional integrity of the system and the perceived strategy become compromised.

These are just a few of the risks that can attack any long-term systems initiative. Any IT manager could think of ten more in as many minutes. The real point is that the execution of a long-term IT strategy is not as predictable as we might like to believe.

In any organisation IT applications and supporting infrastructure will be in several different stages of maturity. There will be mature systems that have been up and running for several years, scheduled enhancements for these systems both large and small, systems which are being implemented for wider organisational use, small localised systems which may or may not find their way to wider use within the organisation and systems which are being evaluated as to their suitability for one function or another. The situation will be further complicated by various 'infrastructure' projects which will be concerned with rationalisation, integration, cost-effectiveness, performance and availability of the existing systems infrastructure.

To adopt a perspective that all these issues, many of them incomplete, can be tipped into a corporate blending machine so that an all-encompassing step-by-step strategic plan emerges, is impractical to say the least. The real issue in the determination of an IT strategy which supports the corporate mission is that:

- Existing applications are enhanced to continue to support the firm's business operations and planning processes.
- That new applications deliver tangible benefits (by this I mean measurable in the broadest sense of the word, rather than the traditional financial measures).
- That the potential of new technologies and applications is fully harnessed in the pursuit of business goals.

- That the supporting technical infrastructure is optimised on the required price/performance, responsiveness and quality criteria.

These four points are, of course, the obvious objectives that any organisation would be seeking to achieve through its use of IT. I have to say also that most of the IT managers and their staff are working extremely hard to make this happen. Unfortunately, their efforts are often frustrated, not because of a lack of commitment, skill or expertise, but because the structure of both IT and user departments is not conducive to the ongoing exploitation of IT.

A strategy (whether it is IT, marketing or whatever) is a goal or a mission. But unlike climbing a mountain or breaking the world 1500 km record, you never actually arrive. When the required levels have been attained, you have to stay there, perhaps improve or maybe diverge to other targets. In essence, a strategy never starts nor finishes, it is a continual guiding philosophy which (should) guide short-, medium- and long-term decisions and actions. The essence of the problem then, is not the provision of an all-encompassing script to be learned by rote and mechanistically operated by all individuals within the company. The key issue, and particularly with IT, is mobilisation. It is the concept of providing an environment where IT-related initiatives can be evaluated and acted upon quickly and effectively. For IT to be exploited, there needs to be a free flow of information, positive consideration of new ideas, a commitment to learning, a willingness to experiment and a continual exposure to issues and events which occur outside the company.

From Concept to Strategy – A Case Study

I like case studies – they make concepts come alive. The case study which follows summarises the experiences of the Britannia Building Society with Document Image Processing (DIP). I must emphasise that the nature of the technology is largely irrelevant; it is the evolutionary nature of the project itself which offers the greatest gems of wisdom.

Briefly, DIP is a technology which allows the capture, storage and retrieval of source documents via computer. The concept is analogous to storing a photocopy on disk. With the capacity of optical disks the attraction of significantly reduced storage space alone is enough to warrant the interest of many companies in DIP. DIP systems also come in various 'flavours', ranging from retrieval systems based on predetermined indices, to complex systems which can automate and monitor workflows. The personal financial services industry with its paper-generating capabilities is therefore a potentially fruitful candidate for the introduction of DIP.

But DIP is a relatively new technology and we have little experience of the organisational consequences of introducing it.

The Britannia Building Society had always had a concern regarding the paper storage problems that come with 250 000 mortgage accounts. Earlier experiences with microfilm-based systems had failed to fulfil the Society's requirements, hence the paper-based system continued. However, in 1986 the Society began a pilot scheme with DIP which involved its mortgage completion, insurance and securities departments.

The first point to notice is that while certain technical solutions (i.e. microfilm) were discarded, the concept of some form of electronic document capture and the potential benefits still remained a principle.

The pilot-scheme started with just twenty terminals which were given to key staff in each section. By giving a number of staff from different sections a chance to operate the system the maximum benefit was gained from a small pilot-scheme. This allowed the potential organisational changes to be experienced in a controlled manner.

The new technology can be tested for many different applications, but still in a localised and controlled environment. The system though widely dispersed over the user base did not at first process significant volumes. The users – unpressured by tight, highly visible and critical deadlines – could learn about the system over time. By 1988 the system had proved its capabilities and potential, and all sixteen sections of the mortgage function were brought on to the system.

By now, business issues and ongoing experience with the system were shaping the Society's perspective towards DIP. Based on its previous experience with DIP, the Society realised that future DIP systems really needed to be of the more sophisticated case-related type if the Society was to get the most benefit from it.

Experience is a powerful tutor. Now the Society was in a position to refine its strategy on the basis of knowledge rather than assumption.

Case-related DIP systems are particularly useful in insurance applications where completion documents can be accessed by reference to a common client-file. The shortcomings of the current system where 40 per cent of the paper-based files were unavailable at any given time, and consequently affecting customer service, brought DIP into a different perspective. A joint exercise between the records management and R&D functions produced a business case which was submitted to senior management.

Note how the capabilities of DIP have been associated with the high-level business need to speed up access to documents and improve customer service. This is true strategic alignment.

After receiving approval from management, a more formalised approach to implementation was adopted. The Society focused on DIP-supported workflow applications rather than the simpler storage and retrieval approaches used earlier. The workflow applications are now seen as a catalyst for change, capable of supporting new and radical organisational structures and other paper-intensive areas of the Building Society are now being reviewed. Consideration is also being given to networking the system to branches.

The Society has gradually perceived greater and greater benefits to be derived from this project by taking maximum advantage of their learning experiences.

By now the project is beginning to look more like the archetypal strategic development project. The technical infrastructure planning, requests for capital approval and formal management disciplines are in place. But the project did not start out that way – it evolved. From some humble beginnings DIP has emerged as a mission-critical system as a result not of the formal methods that were in use but of the vision of the people that were involved and the culture of the organisation that enabled them to achieve that vision. The structured, formal stuff came later – when the business benefits could be seen.

In this case it was the records manager at Britannia Building Society who, after seeing the pilot system in operation, saw the additional potential of workflow systems. This concept, aided and abetted by the other specialist skills of her colleagues, allowed a convincing business case to be put together. This had nothing to do with method – it was talent – a talent for spotting opportunity.

EVOLUTION NOT REVOLUTION

Figure 5.1 represents the way that strategic information systems may emerge. They may not always happen this way

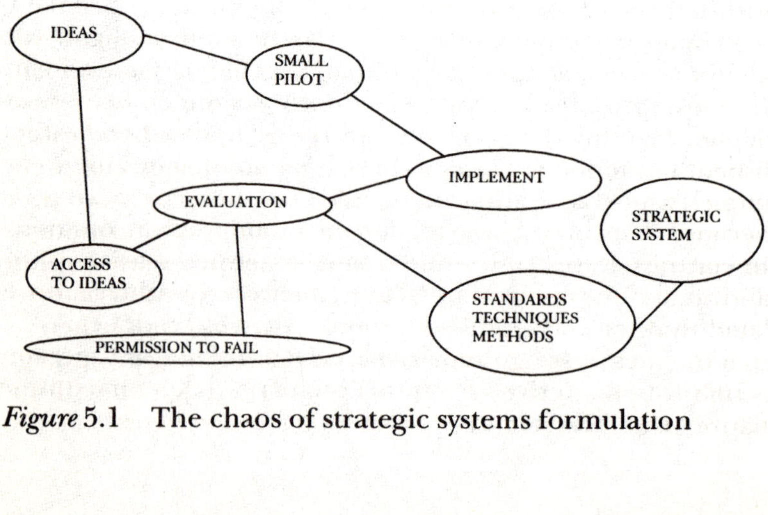

Figure 5.1 The chaos of strategic systems formulation

but most often do, particularly if they are based on technologies which are new to the organisation.

While standards and guidelines could conceivably be defined for pilot projects, evaluating pilot projects, generating alternative solutions and even generating ideas these would not in themselves provide the answers. The real catalyst within this is the nature of the people involved and the manner in which the organisation facilitates their efforts.

ENTER THE INFOPRENEUR

In the end, it turns out to be down to *people* after all! Despite all the techniques and technological gizmos it turns out that knowledge and vision are the real engines of transformation.

Why people? It is because people are at the extremities of an organisation, at its interfaces with customers, suppliers and its markets. It is also people who interact at the functional interfaces within an organisation, such as sales/marketing, production/marketing, R&D/production. It is at these interfaces where internal processes are re-engineered, customer preferences and behaviour noted. If we accept that a firm's strategy is shaped and reshaped by external events, then it must be that those feeling the effect of those events will perceive the potential opportunities that lie within them – if they have the vision.

People with vision and who are committed to progress will always succeed where pure methods and techniques will fail. In most cases, their commitment to pursuing this vision allows them to transcend current paradigms and the established, conventional wisdom. The methodologies and techniques which were discussed earlier can never achieve this, because their application in an organisation is intermittent. In contrast, the possession of a flexible mind, focused vision and an ability to forge new linkages between previously unrelated things is a continuous process. The difference then, is that the methodology approaches to determining IT strategy is only illuminating for a one-off moment. It is a one-off initiative in the pursuit of opportunity. Infopreneurs, on the other hand, perpetually seek opportunity and change. It is as if they can receive the same signals from their environment and interpret them differently and almost simultaneously. Over and above responding to the more mundane day-to-day issues, they can filter out other information (which may be anything from a new/changed technology to a business problem) and spot an IT-related opportunity or solution.

It is then, the infopreneurs who cause transformation via information systems. Indeed, most methodologies which have been formulated by studying the activities of other companies merely serve as a historical record of infopreneurial activity. Our 'holy grail', if we can now call it that, lies not in techniques but in the thought processes and activities of certain individuals. Organisations must now accept that they need to find and mobilise these individuals.

THE UNIFIED APPROACH

Throughout this book thus far I have tried to present several perspectives on information, IT and the nature of corporate innovation related to IT deployment. To summarise this and to put it in the context of strategy implementation, we are confronted with a situation as follows:

- The ways in which information can be used, when liberated by IT, are almost limitless.
- There is no one right way to direct the strategic investment in IT – although there are several useful perspectives we may choose to adopt.
- None of the published case studies in the strategically significant use of IT followed 'traditional' techniques. On the admission of the implementors, no formal methodologies were employed, and the nature of the technology used was not a decisive factor.
- We continue to learn more about the potential application of IT over time. This learning never stops.
- Innovation can occur at any time and any level within the organisation – it cannot be conveniently summoned

forth at the time we choose to formulate a grand master plan.

- Information innovation comes from certain individuals within the organisation.

Clearly, a different approach is necessary – one that relies less on technique but which concentrates more on harnessing those innovations that do occur (and most likely are occurring) into action and implementation; one which creates an environment which significantly increases the probability of these innovations occurring.

In adopting a holistic approach to IT strategy, we can achieve the elusive integration and obtain an even greater prize – unification. Unification occurs when business thinking and IT thinking become inseparable. They become one and the same thing.

To achieve all this, we have to adopt a principle which at first may make us somewhat uncomfortable – particularly the deterministic IT practitioner: *we cannot predetermine the future by detailed analysis.* The words of John Naisbitt in *Megatrends* strike an original note:

> The gee-whiz futurists are always wrong because they believe that technical innovation travels in straight lines. It doesn't, it bobs and weaves and lurches and splutters...

The same is true of information innovation. Most IT departments have a good understanding of the long-term infrastructure issues, that is, the technical infrastructure that is likely to form the platform which might support the future business systems. Expected price-performance trends, facilities available from hardware and software suppliers can, in the main, be analysed and predicted. But precisely what the applications may be is dependent on the unpredictable occurrence of lateral thought and this cannot be preordained. And seeing how technology may be applied or information used in support of a business mission is precisely the process of lateral thinking, connecting two things that may have been previously unconnected.

The issue is directly related to John Naisbitt's observations. Whilst technical capacity can be forecast, how it may be applied cannot. And when applications are perceived, they will occur at places and times within your organisation that will be indeterminate and random. The five-year IT strategy is dead in terms of forecasting IT usage. Whilst we may accurately forecast technological trends in terms of abstract capacity we must accept that we cannot forecast potential applications. We need to resist the 'tramlines' mindset whereby the future of IT use is pre-ordained in advance, and accept that significant applications may be perceived at any time.

In order to achieve this we must radically rethink our approach to thinking strategically about IT. This level of thinking must exist on a continuum at all levels within an organisation (because learning is not confined to rank) and must be harnessed and distilled on a continuous basis. This cannot be achieved by annual or biannual studies and bland reports circulated throughout the organisation. It has to be something to which all levels of the organisation can contribute on an ongoing basis, day in, day out, and be enabled by a supportive organisational process which turns ideas into working systems.

Traces of these principles are emerging in some organisations which have recognised that 'information innovation' is something which is enacted by individuals, not technique, and is made possible by organisational culture rather than by process or method.

6 Technology Transfer: The Key to Alignment

Any business-driven IT strategy consists of several aspects, predominantly consisting of a business requirement for an information system and a technological base for such a system. In between these two major components is a grey area, which is predominantly a thought process. This aspect of strategy formulation can be termed the *technology transfer process*, which generally occurs in one of two ways:

- The features or attributes of a particular technology are seen to enable a business initiative which contributes in some way towards the firm meeting its goals or objectives.
- A business initiative is perceived to have a valid information systems content – one which will either contribute knowledge (that is, by analysing information, thus supporting decisions), enable some kind of service, or support internal processing efficiencies.

These are not generally the outcome of formal strategy studies; such initiatives tend to fall into an approach of technical forecasting. Technical forecasting tends to look at IT usage within the confines of vertical growth and ask the question 'How much more?' Thus issues such as network bandwidth, new platforms and development tools are the major considerations, concentrating on the issues of price, capacity, performance and responsiveness. Here the deterministic mindset of the IT professional is exploited. The process of technical forecasting lends itself well to stepwise logical analysis. Based purely on the organisation's broad view of its future structure and business volumes, a complementary technical infrastructure can be determined in a fairly straightforward manner. For instance, a move towards decentralisation would imply a need for additional networking to allow access to a central IT installation. Thus, based on existing and projected business volumes, a reasonable strategy can be defined which incorporates the necessary technologies and changes to existing systems, procedures and operating practices. This would eventually form a reasonable IT strategy which would support the initiative of decentralisation.

For an IT department not to conduct such an exercise regularly is unthinkable. A well-planned, responsive IT infrastructure is essential for most firms, except perhaps the smallest (and even this is debatable). The problem with the type of strategy studies mentioned above is that they deal only with the consequences of a given initiative, they do not contribute to extending a firm's capability to exploit the capabilities of its IT systems.

The concept of technology transfer is far less predictable in its nature and is best described as opportunistic applications-spotting, rather than an analytical process. It is the process of 'seeing' an IT-related business opportunity rather than rigorously grinding it out of some kind of predetermined procedure. The problem is that a significant contention lies between a need for opportunistic, spontaneous idea generation and the need for a stable, long-term plan to provide an effective IT infrastructure.

In fact, both are needed. The technical forecasting aspects are required to provide a coherent, cost-effective and responsive technical infrastructure. Technology transfer is a major component in extending a firm's overall capabilities in terms of its competitive position, cost structure and overall capital productivity. Take away the technical forecasting element and technical chaos is likely to ensue with a proliferation of incompatible equipment and software. Company experience during the early days of corporate personal computing and of the widespread devolution of IT responsibility to user departments attests to this risk. On the other hand, concentrating solely on the technical forecasting element of IT has been shown to produce a sterile 'technocratic' environment in which systems decisions are made on a purely technical basis, with little or no consideration of business imperatives.

Most firms manage the technical forecasting elements reasonably well. Existing frameworks of supplier liaison, technical evaluations of new IT products, performance and capacity management, change controls and the prospecting approaches adopted by IT suppliers allow a forward-looking IT function to keep 'in tune' with technical trends. However, the concept of technology transfer is proving far more elusive for it is not a methodical process but one which occurs randomly and unexpectedly.

THE NATURE OF TECHNOLOGY TRANSFER

Technology transfer is primarily the process of conceiving of new linkages between a firm's activities, information and the capabilities of information technology (IT). It occurs initially in the mind, not on paper, and is the result of some external stimulus, encountered within or around the working environment. This may then trigger off a conceptual linkage between technological capability, a business problem or opportunity and the information related to that opportunity. The process, if that is what it can be called, was generally described by Martin Gardner in *The Scientific American* in his article 'Aha! Insight': 'The sudden hunch, the creative leap of the mind that "sees" how to solve a problem in a simple way ...'

Herein lies the key to the exploitation of IT. The answer lies not within the nature of the technology itself, nor in the pure analysis of all the different types of information within a company. It is not in the methodical cross-matching of business initiatives to a technological equivalent which creates a significant IT innovation, but in the ability to transcend all these individual considerations and determine new and potentially valuable linkages. This is where 'methodologies' such as 'Customer Resource Lifecycle', 'Re-engineering' and 'IT for Competitive Advantage' appear so tantalising, yet so difficult to emulate. The reason why so many of the companies who employ them fail is because they are seduced by the apparent ease by which they can be emulated. They fail to appreciate (and so, too, do their protagonists) that the methodology is based on the outcome of initiatives taken by organisations whose case studies support various aspects of the methodology. The fundamental issues which most ignore is how the initiatives were born in the first place. All the major approaches to formulating a business-driven IT strategy grossly oversimplify the chaotic and random nature of this type of innovation.

Technology transfer starts its life as an idea, the creator of which may have little technical knowledge, but a conceptual understanding of capability. That idea is the result of four, often simultaneous, thought-processes which may be categorised as *Probe, Transcend, Project* and *Join* (see Appendix to this Chapter). They can briefly be described as the act of looking at the big picture, considering an alternative based on a perception of capability and the establishing of one or several linkages between the capability and a requirement.

Within these relatively simple statements lies a universal truth – that is not as easy as it appears. The fact of the matter remains that although the identification of new linkages between technology, information and a firm's business can be summarised in these four words, both the stimulus and the elements from which these innovations flow are just not visible to most organisations. In the words of Martin Heidegger, the German philosopher ... 'We stand in the realm of that which hides itself ...'

Information is all around us, as familiar as the air we breathe. Like air, we take it for granted and therefore often fail to think about it and see other uses for it. Information is both passive and subsumed within our daily work life. Consequently we tend to view it only through the perspectives provided by current systems. These systems – used daily – within the organisation tend to confer a certain permanence on both the structure and use of the information. But, of course such information structures, relationships and uses are not fixed, they just happen to be the ones we currently use. Other uses may indeed exist, if we knew how and where to look for them. For instance, if a system maintains information by category, how many people would consider investigating whether the subcategories could be identified by analysing activity within two previously unrelated categories? Yet it was this exercise which instigated Wells Fargo Bank's highly successful demographic marketing strategy. The key to exploiting information lies not in massive exercises of data analysis but in constant probing, inquiry and evaluation. One reason that the massive corporate data-base projects fail to deliver tangible benefit is not because the concept of wide availability of data or information is a flawed concept. It is primarily because the usage and the nature of the decisions to be drawn from it are often vague and the system provides information based on traditional rather than new perspectives. To exploit information over and above current use requires it to be viewed outside current perspectives.

As information is subsumed within the fabric of a firm so are its systems subsumed in terms of the way things are done. The majority of systems within a company were introduced as a means to increase efficiency, rather than extend capability. Their function was to perform existing tasks faster, rather than to enable additional functions to be undertaken. Again, they are taken for granted, as familiar as are the train and the car as a means of getting to and from work.

The reason why so many companies fail to capitalise fully on their IT investment has very little to do with the technical competence of their IT function nor the competence of user management. Their primary failing lies within their inability to foster new perspectives on the use of IT. Hence, when one or two competitors catch them 'on the hop', they tend to amass behind the latest methodology in an attempt to emulate their competitors. This is the quick-fix mindset which dogs so many managements and is not restricted to IT-related matters. Alluring methods and techniques which are peppered with examples of successful companies to support their 'how to' instructions, provide only a superficial glimpse of the real issue. You cannot learn how to swim from a book – you have to get into the water and get wet. Whilst specific examples of exploiting IT can be copied by the many, the few who lead will stay in the lead. Technology transfer, the key to the exploitation of IT is not something which can be done or enacted by following a procedure.

Rather, it is a practice which is advanced and encouraged by the nature of a particular organisation.

WHY TECHNOLOGY TRANSFER DOES NOT ALWAYS HAPPEN

The problem of achieving radical performance gains via IT, harmonising it with business strategy or generally making it contribute towards the organisation's goals is that alternatives to existing methods must be somehow generated. It is therefore necessary that, at all levels within the organisation, a degree of thinking outside current boundaries is constantly occurring. Bringing IT into the picture can make the issue even more abstract. IT is passive, of itself it offers no obviously inherent capability. That capability must be known and subsequently associated with improving some value-adding activity of the organisation or provide some new and useful knowledge which will allow improvements to be made. Thus, the reason many organisations fail to realise the full capability of their IT investments is because they adopt initiatives that are diametrically opposed to creative thinking.

The search for a prescriptive 'how to' method is in conflict with the true nature of information innovation. Systems will not become strategically aligned by one-off reviews, evaluations or projects. The process of honing and harmonising existing systems and acquiring new ones to support a business mission is a perpetual and an habitual process. It has to be this way as the changes which affect a firm's operating environment are equally restless and perpetually changing. Vertical, straight-line thought-processes will never succeed in this environment.

In order to maintain control and achieve day-to-day operating efficiency all organisations need to operate according to preconceived, predefined manner. This is, of course necessary in order to ensure that the organisation runs smoothly. But these systems become ingrained within the organisation and tend to be considered as the only method of doing things. Hence when implementing new IT systems, they tend to be configured around the same pattern rather than in alternative patterns that the new technology may be able to support.

What is required, then, is not another stepwise process of analysis. To see and create new ways of conducting work, serving our customers better and managing our business more effectively we need to foster innovative systems thinking.

A NEW MINDSET AND A NEW ATTITUDE ARE REQUIRED

Our previous attempts to emulate the vanguards of IT exploitation have been supported by techniques that are too simplistic and do not address the real issue, which is why some firms seem consistently to extend the use of IT and its contribution to their business vision. Studying these companies to determine the secret attributes of their success is a fascinating (and potentially financially rewarding!) task. However, merely studying the outcome of their endeavours will impart nothing of the thought-processes which conceived the idea. A study of the actions of any particular entity will yield little information in respect of why it acts that way and what causes that behaviour. Consider, if you will, in the field of natural history, a study of the hunting process of a tiger. By studying only how a tiger kills its prey will yield little knowledge of all of the attributes which make this animal a master hunter. By studying the outcome of its actions (the actual kill) several conclusions could be drawn; a master hunter needs long teeth, strong jaws, physical strength and speed. These conclusions, though correct, would be so incomplete as to create a fallacious concept. They would ignore the more subtle attributes of an animal in harmony with its environment via its highly developed sense of sight, smell and hearing, its physical characteristics of natural camouflage and stealth. For it is these characteristics which allow the animal both to sense its prey and approach it, undetected, until it becomes close enough to strike.

Firms which lead in the use of IT seem to achieve their successes by a means similar to that described above. Their significantly enhanced use of IT is not achieved by following a prescribed procedure, but rather as a predator senses that his prey is nearby. For these companies, IT innovation is more a way of life rather than a closely guarded technique which is periodically employed. These companies by some form of nervous system are able to sense an opportunity to apply IT whether it is presented within a business initiative, a new perspective on information use or the capabilities of recently extended or new technology.

These are issues that run far deeper and require a broader understanding than the *ad hoc* study of the outcome of a particular set of initiatives can ever hope to achieve. In the study of the design and manufacturing initiatives taken by Jaguar plc in their development of the XK 220 the following appeared in the *International Journal of Vehicle Design*:

> In order to understand how technological changes come about at company level requires paying attention not just to the scientific or technical origins but [also to] the range of organisational and managerial factors involved. The essence is that business performance has always been contingent on both new products, processes and ways of organising ...

The implications for the exploitation of information technology are clear; that the successful actualisation of information (via IT) is contingent not only on the availability of such technology to store and process it. The fundamental source of information exploitation comes from the focused interaction of an overall set of capabilities such as technical expertise, business skills, knowledge, objectivity and a willingness to accept and manage change. To exploit IT fully, a firm does not necessarily need method of process (these are more appropriately employed during implementation), it needs a different mindset. There are no panaceas out there, no methods that can be prescriptively employed at a particular moment in time to provide a quick fix.

The business community at large is accepting the concept that detailed planning of activities, years in advance, will be based on assumptions that will be quickly invalidated. The business environment is just too volatile. A firm's strategy is an ongoing iterative process which is continually prodded, poked and influenced by external political, economic, social and technological ('PEST') factors. A firm's attention to changes in these factors prompts its response to changes in them in the form of identified opportunities and tactical initiatives. If, therefore, a firm's business strategy is shaped in such an unpredictable manner, information-systems deployment to support the business will need to occur in a similar manner. Hence, information-systems deployment will be evolutionary, chaotic and random, not prescriptive, and be functionally, rather than technically, driven.

A management team must therefore accept several fundamental concepts before a firm can adequately galvanise itself to become 'information-driven'.

1. Strategic moves, whether they involve information systems or not, will always be refined, change direction or be superseded as the business, competitive and technical environment changes. From new information systems further opportunities may arise and others will have to be revised.
2. Hardware, software and information of themselves confer no value. The attainment of a high-performance information-driven organisation is the consequence of a well-informed, highly interactive organisation.
3. Company culture plays its part by encouraging new ideas, giving the 'mavericks' headroom, allowing new ideas to rise up and circulate quickly.
4. A commitment to building responsive IT departments which can deliver quality solutions within a sound technical architecture.

Having accepted that these are the prerequisite concepts to harnessing and exploiting IT, a firm must then set about building the necessary attributes to make itself responsive, outward-looking and innovative. These things do not come packaged; the best a company can do is to increase the probability of them occurring. It is time for managers and organisations to discard their search for the ultimate panacea. Innovative, new and radical uses of IT do not spring from the pages of expensive manuals. They are the result of learning, probing, relearning and opportunism. The need is not for new methods and procedures but for new organisational processes and attitudes. In essence organisations need to re-evaluate completely the way in which they identify new and extended IT applications and harness the potential capabilities of new technologies. What is required is that formal, methodical approaches are supplanted by an almost habitual process of searching, investigation and evaluation.

APPENDIX: THE FOUR ELEMENTS OF TECHNOLOGY TRANSFER

1 Probe

The constant process of search and investigation into potentially useful applications of IT. The direction of investigation may be random, driven by a press article, a casual conversation or attending a demonstration of a new system or technology. It is fuelled by unstructured information flows not by formal presentations or seminars. This is the motivational aspect of technology transfer – it is a mindset that accepts that 'there is always something out there' and an attitude that actively seeks it out.

This is the first and most important step – the one that actively seeks opportunity rather than passively waits for opportunity to present itself. It is a daily activity and is not called into play only when required by a formal study.

2 Transcend

The consideration of the 'big picture', how the concepts and principles obtained from researching and investigation activities might fit in to an organisational activity or process. This is the formative stage where a conceptual application is born as the technology is mapped onto an organisational function. This stage is the conceptualisation of the potential use of a new technology or a different view of information.

3 Project

This is the formative stage of a potential application where its organisational fit is conceived and the potential benefits envisaged. The potential processes become clarified as do the required changes. Assumptions may be challenged and new working methods envisaged. This stage is where detailed business knowledge becomes imperative as conventions, market practice and feasibility are all simultaneously challenged as the initiative is considered and verified.

4 Join

As the concept becomes firmer and more capable of description, implementation options are considered and proposals drafted. Now likely to involve several individuals, focused on the proposal or concept, this stage marks the transition from conceptual, opportunistic and iterative thinking towards the more formal implementative disciplines.

7 Ways to Recognise Infopreneurs

> It is not the suppliers of information technology who deliver the results from automation. In each organisation there is a group of individuals – high performance people – who are the agents of change. It is they who facilitate the transformation which takes full advantage of computers.
>
> Paul A. Strassman, *Information Payoff*

WHY INFOPRENEURS MAKE THE DIFFERENCE

Anyone with entrepreneurial capability, regardless of specific vocational skills, displays one particular ability – a 'nose' for an opportunity. This comes from a capacity to see things from a different perspective or, perhaps more importantly, to see the relevance of something previously unrelated to an existing situation. It is, in essence, the epitome of lateral thinking or – as psychologists refer to it – spatial intelligence. It is this power of association – the connection of two or more things that were previously unconnected – that makes the difference.

This personal attribute is the catalyst which enables investment in IT to be capitalised to its fullest extent. This exploitation is the differential between mediocre use of information systems and above-average or leading use. However, this exploitation may not come in the form of a significant strategic information system. It will also show itself as many small improvements in mundane day-to-day systems. The deciding factor in the initial conceptualisation of new and improved applications lies not within the technology installed but in the innovative capabilities of the people using it: 'the root of the advantage is a difference in skills ... It's a problem of fundamentally changing the business and of developing a new set of skills from the shop-floor to the executive suite that are needed to be successful in the new business ...' (John Cecil and Michael Goldstein, 1990).

This quotation emphasises my point; however, in my opinion the issue is somewhat broader. Using IT strategically has brought significant business benefits to several major organisations, as we have already seen. However, the effect of many small exploitations of IT occurring at all levels throughout the organisation is an equally powerful catalyst for change. There is also the concept of chain reactions, which accounts for two major issues related to the emergence of strategic information systems:

- They are often derived as extensions of current systems performing mundane, routine tasks.
- They have small, humble beginnings until the potential for them is seen

These chain reactions occur where there is a convergence between strategic business thinking and the potential of current systems and information to fill a gap. It is not so much the methods employed as the person employing them.

The problem that so many companies face is that they just do not know who infopreneurs are, or for that matter how to recognise them. Many infopreneurs lie latent within an organisation with their talents and initiative confined only to their own work space. Herein lies the key to the problem of realising ongoing benefit and return-on-investment from IT. The major restriction of the effective use of IT is not a company's ability to implement a given technology or understand its principles of design and operation but its inability to envisage new, innovative and beneficial applications for it.

Identifying new IT applications (as opposed to replacing old systems with new ones) is not a process that can be proceduralised, prescribed, ordained or legislated for. Seeing new uses of information and systems whether at localised level or organisational, strategic level, is the practice of innovation. Embracing and nurturing the various occurrences of IT-related innovation is something which very few organisations are in a position to do. Innovation, or plain old-fashioned good ideas are not just the province of R&D; it occurs all over the organisation, in different locations and at different levels. Hence in order to make the best use of its infopreneurs, a company must first learn to recognise and identify them. Unfortunately, this is easier said than done. Entrepreneurial capability is not recognisable by physical attributes (i.e. colour of eyes, hair) nor by the possession of educational qualifications. A good many famous entrepreneurs have been typified by their lack of success (or experience) in traditional organisational cultures, and their lack of formal qualifications. An entrepreneur is recognised primarily by certain attributes of his/her behaviour and mindset; an infopreneur is precisely the same.

THE MINDSET OF INFOPRENEURS

Infopreneurs adopt a broad view on markets, technology, their company and how their activities are influenced by changes in these things. They are aware of opportunities and imperatives posed by changes and developments in these areas and may demonstrate this by submission of unsolicited papers, reports, casual conservations and observations during meetings.

Infopreneurs are able not only to observe change, they assimilate the implications of it and will propose technology-based solutions and directions to capitalise on it. Note that these suggestions may not always fit in with the perceptions of their management!

While infopreneurs are confident of their knowledge and abilities, they will rarely indulge in 'ivory tower' thinking. They are incessant builders of both formal and informal networks, both to receive information and get things done. They continually seek further information, not because they are afraid of not knowing but because they always seek to know more.

Infopreuners are often futurists; they look to, and often try to predict, the future in generic and conceptual terms.

They are also capable of broad thinking about the organisation as a whole – what a change 'here' might do to the way things are done 'there'. This is a demonstration of the infopreneur's capability of lateral thought, sometimes called 'helicopter vision'. This particular attribute, in an internal study by Shell UK, was identified as the only consistent differential between highly effective and only marginally effective managers.

Infopreneurs are not 'passive' learners. Knowledge for knowledge' sake has little part in their credo. They will seek to understand all that they consider to be relevant to their current vision and to reaffirm that it is correct. They tend to favour active, 'how to', learning, rather than formal technical courses. It is they who generally ask 'how to' in order for them to progress to the next stage of their vision.

Infopreneurs constantly seek improvement. They will incessantly refine, revise, extend and re-evaluate their efforts. Once one skill has been mastered, one step taken, their focus will shift to the next issue until time or circumstance sets off a trigger to improve what has gone before.

In order to recognise infopreneurs we need to recognise them by their behaviour. The above discussion on the mindset of an infopreneur describes their ethos, credo or personal *raison d'être.* In fulfilling their own particular missions, the infopreneur will display certain, though not necessarily all, of the behaviours listed below. Broadly speaking, infopreneurs are the IT equivalent of the 'informed opportunists' which Peters and Waterman identified as the essential factor in driving excellent companies further forward.

The term 'informed opportunists' is so significant and so apt, that it warrants further consideration. You could use the phrase 'knowledgeable doer' for this paints a picture of action. Essentially, infopreneurs or informed opportunists bring knowledge and action together in order to achieve change. By keeping 'informed' they sustain knowledge about their company, its markets, its systems and its goals and the relative implications of developments in one sphere to the other spheres. Their opportunism is demonstrated when they identify ways in which to capitalise on these developments in order to bring about initiatives which achieve their company's goals. Infopreneurs do this with IT at both macro and micro level.

HOW TO RECOGNISE AN INFOPRENEUR

Infopreneurs are in every organisation and at all levels. In order to develop them and maximise on their potential, an organisation must first be able to recognise them. Most organisations now have a performance management system of one kind or another in order to evaluate the effectiveness and contribution of their employees. Of these companies, only a handful evaluate their employees on their use of IT. Even those that do tend to focus on IT proficiency (whether as a particular technical specialist or end-user) within the confines of their current functions, rather than their ability to envisage new and different uses for the technology. Even taking into account the relative newness of IT, I find the frequent chief executive statements of their firm's commitment to IT a complete paradox to the scant and rudimentary techniques that these companies use to measure the capabilities of their personnel in this area.

The problem is that you cannot identify a potential infopreneur by his age, education or professional qualifications. The difference lies not much in what they are but in the manner in which they undertake their work.

Typical Behaviours of an Infopreneur

Infopreneurs learn – and teach – by example
An infopreneur is a self-motivated learner and continually follows up leads. Sometimes these will be searches for a specific solution – 'How can I get the system to do this?' – or they may be due to a more holistic search for knowledge and understanding on which he may capitalise at a later stage.

An inforpreneur, though confident of his ability, will consider his involvement with IT as an ongoing apprenticeship – a continuous learning process. An infopreneur will act both as mentor and pupil, showing his colleagues new techniques and facilities whilst learning about new facilities and techniques from other colleagues.

Infopreneurs encourage and subsequently flourish in an environment where informal training is encouraged. Their ongoing search for new knowledge, new applications, is facilitated by an open learning environment where new skills can be learned, new knowledge assimilated and passed on.

Excessive compartmentalisation and formality stifle infopreneurs. Environments which create 'high priests' who perform perfunctory review and approval processes kill off the inquisitiveness of infopreneurs. Though they, too, may be high priests they see themselves as spreaders of their gospel – not guardians of their knowledge. Maintaining a high degree of interaction and a positive consideration of new ideas is critical to maintaining the interest of infopreneurs.

Infopreneurs find new uses for current systems

Employing current systems for uses never previously envisaged is a sure sign that an infopreneur is in evidence. The Wells Fargo and Caterpillar Tractor case studies are instances of this (see Chapter 4). In both cases the systems were put to uses vastly different from those for which they were originally developed; because the information contained in them was considered in a different light.

Infopreneurs often find cheaper ways of doing things by using simpler equipment and software or by combining two or more hardware/software components in new ways. Requests to exchange information between applications or to provide upload capabilities to PCs reflect the machinations of the infopreneur's mind.

In their search for new and expanded uses for their systems, infopreneurs will search for information from various sources. Files containing press cuttings, sending off reader-response cards from magazines, supplier updates and industrial case-studies are telltale signs that an infopreneur is at work.

Infopreneurs train differently

Despite their thirst for knowledge, infopreneurs often shun formal technology training courses. They are happier understanding broad principles and general capabilities and will then turn to experimentation and trial and error, phone calls, conversations with knowledgeable colleagues and so on in the pursuit of their goals.

Manuals are rarely used – only for reference to determine the correct keystroke or confirm understanding of a particular facility.

Infopreneurs quickly assimilate a mental picture of the system and use this, plus the system prompt-and-help facilities (which they expect to be of a high standard – and will complain if they are not) as clues and pointers to help them to achieve their goal. Infopreneurs do not operate by rote learning of manuals and instructions, they use their intuition.

An infopreneur is always likely to be 'first past the post' in a wide range of instances from discovering a new word-processing macro to seeing the potential productivity improvements by, say, image-processing.

Infopreneurs have different measures of performance

Because the infopreneur's credo is one of continuous learning, job enlargement and extension of capability, he often has different views of what constitutes successful performance.

Simplistic production counts will neither impress nor motivate an infopreneur. 'More of the same' does not impress them – 'better than before' is their motto. When appropriate IT will be used to provide *more* or do it *faster*, but the infopreneurs' approach is generally more sophisticated. They tend to drive towards *different ways of doing things* and will consequently consider quality, changing the process by enlarging or re-engineering.

Their commitment to doing this may cause friction among their more cautious peers and supervisors as they challenge conventional wisdom. They will, however, impose much tougher targets on themselves than their supervisors would ever consider and envisage far greater improvements in effectiveness than previously thought possible. Some examples of this may be:

- Programmers who reject lines of code written as an indicator of productivity, pointing to the low levels of repairs and maintenance incurred on programs written using their techniques.
- Customer E-Mail and Electronic Data Interchange (EDI) proposals that result in faster response times and increased accuracy in order-processing.

As infopreneurs look at problems from different perspectives, they also adopt different imperatives and different performance criteria.

Infopreneurs devour information

If your company operates an information-services function that provides access to a wide range of IT-related publications, research material and press-cutting services, try monitoring which individuals regularly use the service. This is a sure-fire way of locating an infopreneur.

Infopreneurs incessantly probe for new developments in the use of IT and these services provide them with a periscope through which to view the outside world. Access to a broad range of information supports the infopreneur's search for new ways to apply IT and to keep up to date with technological developments. Given the opportunity, they will make significant use of any facility which enables them to do this.

By monitoring this you, as a manager, will also get some idea as to how scarce infopreneurs are. In one large organisation of over 50 000 employees, only 1000 felt it appropriate to receive a monthly update of available reports and articles. Of these, only 300 regularly (i.e. more than twice a year) requested copies of the available material. Out of that 300 less than fifty requested something every month – so that is fifty infopreneurs out of 50 000 staff!

One reason for this lies within an individual's personal motivation. Infopreneurs constantly look beyond the boundaries of their current job and will actively seek opportunities to do so.

Infopreneurs enlarge their jobs: they see their career developing horizontally rather than vertically

A somewhat 'chicken and egg' situation, whether infopreneurs are more interested in enlarging their jobs through widening its scope because that is the natural way they work or that they have adapted to the way IT flattens organisations is an interesting academic question. However, the fact remains that infopreneurs do not seek power through seniority. Rather they seek scope and influence by means of undertaking new tasks made possible by harnessing IT.

By bringing information and technology together, infopreneurs not only eliminate repetitive tasks – they generate new work. This work is generally on a different level from the tasks that have been replaced, requiring analytical and interpretive skills. By doing this, infopreneurs redefine and consequently redesign their job so that its scope increases via new tasks and its content may require greater intellectual capacity.

Remuneration of such individuals can be difficult where salary and benefits are determined by grade which in turn has been determined on some points-based system. Infopreneurs buck this system and need to be remunerated by contribution. In many organisations this is often a highly subjective measure as they lack the means to make such measures in a quantifiable and comparative manner. Given the infopreneur's penchant for using measurement criteria different from the historic norm, the issue of an appropriate reward system can be a complex one.

8 Creating an Information Culture

If organisations cannot rely on any one technique, method or any other prescriptive form of approach, what can be done to focus IT investments on improving their business? If there is no universal tool that can be wielded to trim an organisation and its business systems to the desired shape, what other approaches are left to us?

Clearly we cannot just hope for the best. If organisations wish to see their information systems exploited, they must recognise information for what it is – a pervasive and ubiquitous resource. As we have recently established, adopting one view of information (even thought that view may be very useful) cannot hope to cater for all possibilities. Thus any initiatives we choose must be equally as pervasive and ubiquitous as information itself. Organisations must, therefore, first, seek to *influence* the direction and outcome of IT, rather than prescribe precisely what systems should be implemented. Second, a process of continual improvement and evaluation should also be put in place. Organisations change and evolve over time and their information systems should track and contribute to these changes.

In essence, what should be sought after is neither a technique nor a method; it is an overall environment – a culture. Within this culture, guided by clear management messages, exists a perpetual 'keeping in view' of information-systems-related opportunities and improvements. Of course, the intention is not for people to stop working and spend all their time contemplating high-falutin IT applications. Far from it – but what is necessary is that during their day-to-day activities, people are aware of, and see, potential opportunities. The concept is rather like a radio that can simultaneously receive messages on two different frequencies: on one frequency are the routine day-to-day messages, on the other random, intermittent signals that herald opportunities for change and improvement. Underpinning this is an enabling system which actively seeks and draws in ideas, nurtures them and, if appropriate, pushes them through to implementation. Enabling the implementation of ideas is, in many respects, more important than encouraging the actual generation of ideas. For if there is no process in place to progress ideas they will be wasted, overlooked or stifled. Eventually, the very generation of ideas will stop as it becomes 'obvious' that ideas are not really wanted.

To exploit IT thoroughly then, an organisation needs to engender information-systems-thinking throughout itself and at all levels. The following initiatives form individual steps on the journey towards the information culture.

The key issue in exploiting information is that of transferring a technical capability into a business opportunity. This can be difficult for a number of reason:

1. 'Thinking across boundaries' is required from several perspectives. First, there has to be an all-important paradigm shift which sees a situation or information from a different perspective and which relates this to a potential opportunity. Then there has to be a newly established connection between the envisaged solution and the technical capability of IT.
2. There has to be an environment which encourages this kind of thinking, actively supports it, and allows it to progress even if it fails.
3. There has to be a commitment towards learning within the organisation. The principle of 'taking your mind for a run' is particularly apt. People are unlikely to come up with new ideas and IT applications within an insular organisation which is resistant to change. For IT innovation to flourish, there needs to be a constant flow of information regarding new applications of IT, new technologies, etc. Corporate minds will only become active if they are stimulated – continually.

The underlying message of the above list and the issue addressed so far is that there are no 'one-off' outright solutions. Any organisation that truly wants to exploit IT (and consequently still be in business in ten years' time) must recognise that although there may be some useful tools 'out there' it all happens 'in here'. Consequently, the commitment to excellence in IT deployment and usage must be continual.

Using IT effectively is an ongoing learning process. Past experiences provide the opportunity to correct mistakes and build on successes. The emergence of new technologies gives the opportunity to evaluate potential applications. Given the widespread penetration of IT into organisations and the number of different applications, one technique or method cannot be expected to cater for all situations. There needs to be something more than sheer technique to capitalise fully on IT-related opportunities. To achieve this a company must do more than want IT innovation: it must actively encourage and engender a continuous process of technology transfer.

Some leading companies are addressing this issue by taking steps to make themselves more receptive to IT-related initiatives and better able to absorb them. These initiatives, though, are based on organisation rather than on procedures. I believe that they stand a better chance of success than would procedures, because they provide an active catalyst of change – a person. Of course, there has to be an overall environment of enablement to allow the individuals to fulfil their task, but this is at least a step in the right direction. Two distinctly discernible approaches prevail at the moment and interestingly enough are at the two ends of the corporate scale. At one end of the scale there is a specific function within an organisation which draws IT and its users together, which is generically dubbed *the hybrid manager*. At the other end of the scale is the multidisciplinary '*superteam*'. Superteams do not have an organisational 'slot' – in fact they exist to cut across organisational boundaries and implement projects quickly. Both initiatives may provide the environment for the infopreneur but because of their nature will require different roles to be played and provide different accountabilities.

THE HYBRID MANAGER – THE BRIDGE BUILDER

A hybrid manager is seen as a catalyst for integration between the IT and business functions of an organisation. He or she will have both business and IT skills and is responsible for disseminating and implementing IT throughout the organisation. Ten years ago such an idea would have been unthinkable. The IT department, aloof from its user base, stood alone in the organisation, a mini-empire. However, with the increasing trend towards decentralisation of IT and specialised application packages for mini- and personal computers a need for new skills has emerged. Companies who are serious about using IT have realised that they need managers who can straddle the two disciplines and translate business needs to the IT department whilst at the same time anticipate problems and exploit benefits on the end-user side.

Hybrid managers fulfil three key roles in bridging the IT/user divide:

1. *translation.* A hybrid manager can 'speak' the language of both the IT practitioner and of the businessman. In this role he/she can ensure the requirements are unambiguous and understood by both parties, and that solutions meet these requirements.
2. *providing a conduit of all user interaction with the IT department,* so that one user representative can talk to the whole of IT (i.e. operations, development and telecommunications), simultaneously providing a single point of contact for the IT department.
3. '*user husbandry*' whereby the hybrid manager may act as mentor to his user base, helping them to tackle issues such as long-term planning, solving *ad hoc* problems and determining service requirements. Whilst often being seen as a broker, the hybrid manager's prime responsibility is to ensure the most effective use of IT, rather than acting as a buyer or a seller of services.

To date, hybrid managers are born rather than made. Some of the more prominent business schools are offering courses for hybrid managers, and companies such as British

Aerospace and National Power are investing considerable sums in this kind of training. However, in the few companies that do have hybrid managers actively working within them, they have come up through the ranks and are qualified by experience. Whilst their routes to their current positions may vary enormously, most of the current hybrid managers have spent time in both user and IT departments. This would generally have been in 'quality time', in which they have had an extended exposure to both sides of the business. Typical roles that a budding hybrid manager may have fulfilled may be those of project co-ordinator, business analyst or user implementation manager.

Leading companies such as Shell UK, National Power and Saloman Brothers International all have hybrid managers which they call account managers. All operate at high levels within their organisation, each account manager having a number of customers (users) to whom he/she is responsible for solving problems, defining requirements, and managing any problems or changes.

Account Managers need Interpersonal as well as Business and IT Skills

Account or hybrid managers do not have large staffs; they tend to be mainly one-man bands and for this reason need a number of interpersonal skills to do their job effectively. Highly developed skills in negotiating, influencing and diplomacy are all attributes which must be possessed by an account manager – particularly when wide-ranging organisational change is being prompted by them. The account manager is required to act as an envoy between the two areas to stop mistrust and misunderstanding creeping in.

Will Hybrid Managers Make the Difference?

The move towards hybrid managers is a recent one and it may be too early yet to determine whether or not they will be ultimate catalysts of IT-exploitation. A British Computer Society Report on this subject was only recently published (during 1990) and called for 10 000 of these individuals by 1995. Judging by the take-up of this initiative (only a handful of companies had hybrid managers in 1992) it will be some time before there are enough of these managers to draw any conclusions about their overall contribution.

There are, however, a number of pitfalls which should be avoided if hybrid managers are to live up to their expectations. First and foremost, we must be extremely careful not to fall into the 'quick-fix' mode. The hybrid manager is not a Messiah and cannot work miracles. I am sure that there is some mathematical relationship between the amount of press coverage given to an initiative, and management's expectation of its capabilities. As interest in hybrid managers grows, there is a danger that they, too, will become a management fad and the attitude of 'get a hybrid manager, then you can relax' will prevail. If this does occur then the all-too-familiar cycle of euphoria, rising consultancy and recruitment costs, eventually culminating in disappointment will occur.

The second pitfall to be avoided is that of making the hybrid manager a line manager. With line management comes day-to-day responsibilities, internal meetings, procedures, etc. These are not the components of an entrepreneurial environment. They are, of course, necessary for any organisation to function on an ongoing basis but sufficient time and resources should be available to allow the incumbent to stand back and see the big picture. If the function of a hybrid manager is to exploit IT he must be given the opportunity to see new ideas and be exposed to new technologies. Large companies are very good at insulting their employees from the outside world. If this happens to the hybrid manager, then instead of applying IT in new and useful ways, his/her work-load will degenerate to fine-tuning current systems and he/she will become just another cog in a bureaucratic machine.

The third pitfall to be avoided is that of pigeon-holing. A real infopreneur displays behavioural characteristics rather than educational or vocational experience. Years of quality experience cannot be overlooked nor can the need for at least average intelligence be ignored. However, aptitude is not a function of either and until a company has a process in place to locate these people it may find that it is putting the wrong people in the job. Having an educational qualification or several years of experience will help someone to implement IT more effectively, but will not necessarily provide that intuitive 'spark' that results in a new idea. Companies need to be prepared to take hybrid managers from a number of different backgrounds and actively to look for them. Many companies have infopreneurs who would become excellent hybrid managers. However their employers do not know how to find them – or indeed what to look for.

Fourth and last (but by no means least) relates to a previously mentioned issue – hybrid managers, infopreneurs, account managers, call them what you will, are not supermen (or superwomen). They need management support and commitment, they need support systems and above all, an environment which enables them to achieve their goals.

THE SUPERTEAM APPROACH

Many companies, rather than opting for an approach which tries to bring together all the necessary skills in one individual, use multidisciplined teams. The team approach also brings with it one very important benefit, particularly in large organisations, which is the capability to transcend the current organisational structure. Managed properly, these superteams, though small, can make even the largest organisation highly responsive to change.

Many major organisations use the team-building approach to address issues other than IT, and with considerable success. Facilitating change by using the team approach was one of the major differentials between excellent and 'average' companies in Peters and Watermans' book, *In Search of Excellence.* 'The difference made by these switched on teams is not small – it is enormous ...'

One advantage of the team approach is that it is flexible. Teams can be bought together to solve a particular problem or they can be brought together to work over an extended period of time. Small teams tend to achieve more than the might of the whole hierarchy for several reasons:

1. They share a common goal (which may be either short or long term)
2. They tend to have a special status which most individuals find motivating.
3. They can cut across many of the restrictive organisational boundaries that the more formal initiatives cannot.
4. They tend to encourage informal communication between members which can speed up decision-making and subsequent action.
5. Because senior management become involved in sponsoring and enabling these teams, they tend to listen to them!

IT superteams can provide an extremely powerful catalyst of change within an organisation providing that the team mix and supporting environment are there to facilitate their activities. Being a member of a superteam is the ideal place to capitalise on the skills of an infopreneur. Outside formal reporting lines, exposed to different perspectives and fresh ideas, the infopreneur will grow and thrive. The principal benefit to these individuals when working in this environment is 'headroom'. In a team environment an individual can informally present and discuss ideas and receive feedback. Many individuals within organisations have many good ideas but all too little facility to develop and trial them. A good superteam with appropriate sponsorship can provide this environment.

The team approach is conducive to enablement and is an ideal place to try out new tools. Earlier we established that no one model or methodology could provide all the necessary organisational perspective. Given a highly motivated, interdisciplinary team, however, these methods can become powerful tools. Rather then carrying out lengthy formal studies, a team with in-depth knowledge of the business can quickly assimilate the value or otherwise of a particular approach and identify potential applications.

Teams can also provide a fertile environment in which new ideas can grow and be subsequently implemented. They provide a platform from which new ideas can be permeated through the organisation quickly. In this respect, teams can act as the messengers of change, providing a means by which a corporate vision can be translated into something meaningful for all areas of the organisation. Because teams involve people at all levels within the organisation (whether they are inside the team or just working alongside) the message gets through quickly and detailed feedback is obtained, often in an informal manner. Because teams provide the facility to drive new concepts deep within the organisation they also provide an important safety valve. Many of the high-level methods and systematic techniques for determining how things should be done frequently fail to come up to expectations when put into practice. The team approach – providing that the team does not become insular – can get rapid informal feedback on an initiative they may be considering. A quick phone call along the lines 'We're thinking of proposing this – what do you think?' can save thousands of pounds which might otherwise be spent on feasibility studies of analysis requirements, etc.

But probably the most important aspect of superteams is that a multidisciplinary team can be brought together to solve a common problem or reach a consensus decision. This, in my opinion, is the vital link in the unification of IT and business strategy. It is not a methodical process; it is holistic and totalitarian in its approach. For IT to be truly integrated into the strategic and tactical decisions and actions of an organisation, it needs to be understood in terms of products, processes and people. This cannot be achieved by formal procedures, manuals or classroom introduction. You have to get out there and do it.

The Role of Superteams

It would be inappropriate to define what specific issues a superteam should address – the list, in practice, would be never-ending. What I should like to do in this section is to put forward some ideas about the manner in which superteams should conduct their work.

One of the major difficulties facing many organisations is instilling an attitude and ability to transcend the imperatives of day-to-day operations and relate to the longer-term strategic perspective. It is difficult for a distribution manager, faced with meeting dispatch and delivery times, to consider the potential alternatives for re-engineering the processes within his department. Paradoxically, however, it is in the day-to-day environment where the majority of opportunities arise and where the greatest expertise to assimilate the ramifications of such change lie.

One major role of an IT superteam is to act as an agent for promoting alternative thought processes. By keeping abreast of new techniques and approaches the superteam can act as an agent, bringing these new techniques and perspectives to line managers. In an ideal environment, one would expect to see the line managers searching out new techniques and in some companies they do. However, the superteam approach provides a fast-path to providing a level of innovation and questioning in a company, and can act as a stimulus for promoting a higher level of strategic thought.

Superteams should act as an IT think-tank. They should be continually watching and evaluating the capabilities of current and emerging technologies, not from their technical standpoint, but from the perspective of how they are being used. In the same vein they need to consider what applications particular technologies are being used for, both generally and within their business sector. In this respect, superteams become their organisation's eyes and ears, monitoring technological developments in their market sector and technology applications in general. One important aspect to keep in view is that the superteam should not be allowed to dilute itself into a news service. The team's role should be primarily one not of providing information, but of acting as a catalyst for response to external change and opportunities. It is all too easy for the superteam's role to lose its edge and for them to become merely authors of bland reports and sterile presentations. The primary focus of a superteam in this respect is to facilitate response and action in the light of new information, rather than merely to present information.

Monitoring the use of IT by competitors and within the market-place in general is another role the superteam should play. There are two facets to this role: the first is one of ensuring the competitors are not getting ahead or attacking the organisation's markets – which is the basic objective of any competitive intelligence program. The other facet is a little more subtle, which Tom Peters describes as 'creative swiping', that is, using the ideas of your competitors, refining them and improving them. No one organisation has the monopoly on the creative application of IT, so it makes sense to get as many ideas from as many sources as possible.

As more and more technologies become end-user rather than developer orientated, the risk of potential IT opportunities 'falling between the floorboards' increases. The IT practitioner may not see the business value of a particular technology and a line manager may not understand how it could provide a solution for him. A superteam with a number of infopreneurs can provide a powerful platform by which to evaluate and determine the end-user capabilities of a technology. Increasingly, IT products are being marketed to end-users who may have some difficulty in relating them to their day-to-day activities. With the support of an infopreneur, that divide can be bridged. Relating a particular technology to a business problem (or just seeing a potential application opportunity) might occur spontaneously or by formal evaluation. How the initiative is conceived is, however, secondary to the existence of a facility which can actually take it further. In this respect the role of the superteam is to actualise the initiative as well as identify it.

Superteams can and should play a more formal role in an organisation. They can be used to implement major systems, undertake organisational studies for IT application and evaluate packages. This is the more formal aspect of their work which has a finite beginning and end. Although important, project-orientated activities should be only part of the superteam's role and should be considered not as their prime purpose in life but as the outcome of their ongoing activities.

Facilitating IT Superteams

Simply putting a number of people together in a team and calling then an IT superteam will not in itself bring about the desired benefits. The existence of an IT superteam is only one component in a three-part equation. The other two are an enabling environment and a sustaining attitude.

Too many organisational initiatives are seen as one-off exercises, which make a rapid transition from project to procedure. In so many cases, the principles which instigated the project vaporise to nothing as they become translated into process. This is why so many initiatives such as 'customer first', 'total quality', and so on become nothing but hollow words. Even though the manuals, training courses and desktop paraphernalia are in evidence, the all-important principles and attitudes are long gone. If we accept that strategy is in essence a never-ending process in which although certain goals may be met, there will always be new challenges to meet as out external environment changes around us, then we must accept that the establishment of IT superteams to unify IT and business strategy is merely the first step on a never-ending journey.

To achieve this ongoing sustenance the IT superteams must receive regular and ongoing stimulation. This stimulation will come from a variety of sources, such as being given challenging projects and problems, access to external information sources, having time to invest in research and experimentation and having access to your organisation's IT suppliers. While there will be some initial excitement regarding the formation of these teams, the initial impetus and focus must be maintained by management in order to keep the team in step with the organisation. Failure to do this will result in the team involving itself in irrelevant projects, losing direction, and, unable to implement its ideas, it will be likely to drift apart.

Enabling the Team

Whilst IT superteams may be formally initiated (perhaps at a company training centre) facilitating their ongoing interaction is far more important. It is this ongoing interaction over time which sustains the team and maintains its focus.

Provide the teams with significant operational or strategic issues; in other words do not ask them to prepare training courses for word-processing or to generate spreadsheet macros. This is a waste of the infopreneurs' talent. Give them projects with a real challenge, such as improving customer responsiveness by 50 per cent, improving product quality, establishing the application of particular technologies within your market. These groups of high-performing individuals seek to make a significant contribution to their organisation or department; they should not be bogged down with trivial issues that could easily be remedied by installing disciplined working standards.

The type of projects which will appeal to these teams have both depth and breadth, issues which allow them to 'spread their wings' and adopt a broad and unfettered view. Complex problems and projects that clearly contribute to corporate goals are the types of assignment which will get these teams moving.

Committed to high-quality performance, 'Second best isn't worth having' should be their motto. If the outcome of a particular project is measurable against some industry performance criteria (ratio of bad debts to assets for the banking industry, for instance) then use these as project performance criteria. Average performance should never be stated as an objective. If the outcome of a project can be measured in the aforementioned manner (and many can), then the philosophy of 'the average is the worst you can do' should be applied.

Challenging, though realistic, deadlines should be set for project-related activities. Being responsive in today's environment does not mean doing something when you feel like it. The nearer your response time approaches to 'immediate' the more likely you are to stay ahead.

Encourage formal and informal network formations; the continual cross-fertilisation of open minds is essential to organisational renewal. Formal networks can be encouraged by allowing people to form special interest groups within the organisation and join industrial or professional 'task' groups. Informal networks can be promoted by encouraging impromptu gatherings of suppliers and members of other organisations. The wider the focus and the greater the number of stimuli then the greater the amount of knowledge there will be flowing through your organisation.

Encourage visibility; let the whole of the organisation know what the IT superteam is and what it will do. Encourage non-team members to contact it with ideas and questions. A newsletter detailing achievements and providing information on current projects not only maintains its visibility but also further encourages the development of informal networks.

The team should also have visibility with senior management. Ideally it should be able to give regular presentations regarding the progress and results of its work. This has an important two-way benefit; it not only keeps the team and its work visible to its senior sponsors but also demonstrates to the team its sponsors' interest.

Ensure that sponsorship is strong; every IT superteam should have a strong committed sponsor. A group sponsor is primarily responsible for providing an environment which is conducive to success. He or she should provide direction in terms of driving the team's focus towards specific issues and goals. The team sponsor is also the 'corporate middle man'. His responsibility in this respect is that of presenting the organisation's needs to the superteam. Through the sponsor, the organisation's missions and goals can become translated into project-specific objectives focused on the organisation's overall goals.

Overall, the sponsor should act as the guide to the team. While he/she may have no specific responsibilities for project-related tasks, he/she will steer the project to producing an outcome that contributes to the organisation's goals, and will clarify requirements and make corrections to direction if necessary. In addition to providing broad guidance there will also be a responsibility to ensure that appropriate resources are available to support the team's efforts (even capital for pilots of systems or for bench-test evaluations).

Grease the wheels: one of the major advantages of the team-led approach to change management is that it can happen quickly. But this will not happen just because an organisation has teams. Through themselves or their sponsor they must be able actually to do something. This may involve buying-in new software or equipment for evaluation, a prolonged test at a supplier site or running a small pilot. Whilst there are considerations for capital expenditure, it is important that the teams feel empowered to act and that it is demonstrated that they are so empowered. Let them try, and tolerate failure; encourage the team to run small, low-risk pilots whenever possible. The best way to learn about the capabilities of a new technology is actually to use it. If a pilot does not work out, do not disband the team (unless they make a habit of it!). Experience and knowledge are fostered as much by a failure as by a success.

The value of small, self-contained, well-controlled pilot systems cannot be overstated. They form the very basis of familiarisation, allow perceptions to be confirmed and generate confidence in the users. But perhaps even more importantly they provide a platform from which other new ideas may flow.

Demonstrate the team's contribution to them; this is crucial to sustaining the team. When a project has been done well, when the desired outcome has been achieved – let the team know. Of all the motivation techniques available, a sincere word of encouragement must rate as one of the most effective. When a project is completed and has generated the expected benefit, the team should be called back to see its work, and should be congratulated.

Allow solutions to be self-determined; remember that the function of the superteam is to provide IT-related solutions or to capitalise on the potential of a particular technology to business issues. Let the team determine the solution (by virtue of knowledge gained by your company's support system). Do not dictate suppliers without good reason and do not tell them what you want the answer to be. This erodes the feeling of self-empowerment and if it becomes a habit it will demotivate the team from searching for new IT opportunities (what would be the point when the answer to the question has already been determined?)

HYBRIDS VERSUS SUPERTEAMS

Are hybrid managers (a.k.a. account managers) or IT superteams the path to the information culture? To choose one option or another would contradict one of the central tenets of this book – that there is no one right way to manage or apply the strategic application of IT. Closer examination of the two approaches reveals that they perform very different functions.

The hybrid or account manager acts as translator, agent and broker between his user base and IT. His function is neither to innovate nor instigate new applications for his user base. His/her primary function is to manage the supply of that resource, to ensure that it is effectively implemented, cost-effectively delivered and that the solutions meet the users' requirements. The prime function then of a hybrid or account manager is to manage the user's IT resources and expectations for the benefit of the user. It is not to determine how the user should apply IT or envisage new uses.

The IT superteam has a broader and less structured remit. Its work is project-related, rather than operationally orientated and is focused more on shaping the future. The purpose of superteams and the mix of skills within them is to envisage new uses for existing IT applications and new technologies.

I believe that there is a potential and very powerful relationship between the two approaches which, rather than choosing one route or another, calls for both approaches to be combined. By so doing, an organisation provides itself with a powerful IT nerve-centre which may be located deep within the firm's structure.

The hybrid or account manager given appropriate corporate 'clout' makes an excellent sponsor for the superteams. His ability to bridge both the IT and business disciplines makes him the ideal sounding-board for new ideas. His relationship with both users and IT makes him the ideal provider of resources, both human and capital. His organisational relationships provide the necessary platform for actualising new, IT-related initiatives.

Together, the superteam and the hybrid or account manager provide a powerful catalyst for promoting permeating IT-related change throughout an organisation. The IT superteam acts as a stimulus and advocator and, perhaps, ultimate implementor of change whilst the hybrid/account manager acts as the agent and broker for such change.

As I stated before, there is no one right way to exploit IT or to guarantee that it will happen, but with the organisational initiatives I have described in this chapter, the probability of it occurring is greatly increased.

IT superteams, infopreneurs and 'skunk camps' go together. 'Skunk camp' was the term that General Electric Corporation used for the periodic strategic brainstorming exercises which were regularly conducted at GEC. The primary intention of a skunk camp was to bring together individuals from various parts of the organisation to promote and discuss new ideas. Because the necessary individuals were brought together around a common issue – a new product – the progress made at these group meetings is generally recognised as incredible and resulted in a level of responsiveness previously unknown in a company of GEC's size.

This approach is an ideal way to capitalise on the ideas and initiatives of your infopreneurs and provides a means to instigate change quickly. The skunk camp is an ideal forum for the superteam which will subsequently present its ideas to senior management. Skunk camps work for several reasons:

- People swap and refine ideas 'face to face' – communication is informal and the atmosphere promotes supportiveness.

- Lengthy reports containing proposals and alternatives are avoided and hence time is saved.
- People are brought together around a common theme which promotes the teamwork ethos.
- Probably most important, the approach promotes interpersonal interaction. You cannot hide behind memos or reports – you have to get on with it.

Incidentally, GEC is one of the companies included in the survey in Table 5.1 – it does work!

Superteams are not a full-time occupation for anyone – they are part-time. One of the dangers in trying to encourage innovation within a company is that people are given 'innovation' as a full-time role. Consequently they are removed from their normal role – which is where the first spark of innovation often occurs in the first place. Whilst superteam members should get together regularly to work either on particular projects or in a skunk camp, they should not work together full-time on a regular basis. Their stimulation comes from being involved in day-to-day activities, whilst simultaneously keeping a broader perspective in view. Take away the unpredictable stimuli that occur in the day-to-day environment, and their thought-processes are likely to become sterile.

This is one of the greatest challenges in keeping the momentum of IT superteams. They need to be apart so that they have a comprehensive array of experiences, yet they need to get together to brainstorm or implement a particular project.

9 Fourteen Ways to Encourage Infopreneurship

If the exploitation of IT can neither be prescribed or summoned up, must the formulation of strategic system initiatives be left purely to chance? Although an organisation cannot act like a 'short order cook' whenever it is asked to determine a strategic information system, there are a number of initiatives which can be taken in order to stimulate, capture and communicate IT or information-related innovations. As they are presented, the initiatives are focused on end-user application and the organisational outcome of applying IT to produce or process information more effectively or more imaginatively. However, the principles can equally be applied to the technologists within your organisation by changing the focus from using IT more effectively to that of providing high-quality, cost-effective technical solutions.

The prerequisite here is to stimulate an awareness of IT-orientated business opportunities, not to prescribe particular applications. As with most initiatives which involve the response of people, success is not guaranteed. The best that any management can do is to adopt organisational principles which encourage initiative and knowledge-sharing, thereby increasing the probability of success. The suggestions which follow fall into that category, and there is at least anecdotal evidence that the aforementioned probability is significantly increased by their adoption. Attitude is an important ingredient when implementing any or all of the following suggestions; a management team should consider its approach from the perspective of encouraging and enabling innovation rather than attempting to legislate for it. Whilst innovation is likely to occur under certain conditions, intervention will still be required to guide it, capture it and progress it. There can be no let-up because 'the procedure is in place', it requires continual attention and commitment from management. One of the major causes of failure of new management initiatives in many areas of corporate life lies in the lack of post-implementation attention from management.

There is also an element of cultural change implied herein. This requires time to perpetuate and a considerable amount of management-by-example to effect. No organisation becomes innovative overnight but it can take a small step towards that goal every day, providing it sticks to the principles. Thus each of the actions suggested here should be considered as a number of organisational projects, each requiring considerable time and effort to implement them effectively.

But probably the most powerful management motivator for seeking out innovation from all levels in the organisation must surely be the acceptance of 'that's the way it has to be'. The overriding principle is that people at all levels within the organisation should be encouraged to enquire and search continually for new and improved ways of applying IT. The approaches recommended here may prove useful instruments in the creation of such an environment. The uses of information are now so various and versatile that a single perspective will not be good enough. We have seen that models, methods and so on do not, of themselves, make any appreciable difference and that the majority of the significant advances in the application of information technology have come from educated-user areas. We therefore need management systems which stimulate thought, encourage learning and provide a platform for these initiatives and ideas to filter up the organisation rather than allow them to dissipate through its walls.

The initiatives suggested here should not be considered as a quick-fix prescription for one or many maladies associated with the use of IT. Rather, they should be considered as a diet for sustained healthy growth. You cannot just 'do' them and walk away; they are more a way of corporate life which helps you to keep one eye on the future.

CAN IT BE MEASURED?

Measurement criteria can be applied to the proposals which follow – but not financial ones. To attempt to measure the cost of a given initiative against, say, revenue is an invalid measure. But what can be done is to measure in terms of the desired outcome. The ultimate objective is to achieve a more imaginative and effective use of IT by engendering a more innovative environment. Measure, then, the amount of IT-based improvement suggestions, perhaps within categories such as customer service, quality, order-processing, lead-times, etc. In *The Marketing Edge* Tom Bonoma stated that many managers track two or three general measures with which they keep their finger on the pulse of their business. Every business unit or department should know what these key variables area and what affects them. These provide a guiding light against which all IT-related investments may be measured. IT is only the servant of business and its ultimate contribution will occur when its application brings about improvements in these variables. Define these for your business or department, communicate them and then measure, over time, the number of information-orientated innovations related to the improvement of these measures.

ENABLING INFOPRENEURSHIP

1 Keep Close to your Supplier

This applies even to the most humble PC system – not just the major systems. This is a two-way street, with benefits potentially flowing in both directions; a supplier benefits from a demanding user, a user benefits from the supplier's detailed knowledge of their product.

Constant liaison with your supplier provides you with access to a vast knowledge base, which is not restricted to that of the supplier himself but may extend to the whole customer-base of his product. Consequently your budding infopreneurs gain access to two important sources of stimulation:

- from the supplier, in terms of their planned enhancements and extensions of the product;
- specific enhancements which have been requested by other customers and which might be relevant to you.

I have never met a supplier who is not delighted to discuss the capabilities and applications of their product and receive ideas and suggestions about how the use of their product can be extended and enhanced.

Every firm should have a supplier liaison group for every software product in serious use. Where large IT-suppliers are involved, several liaison groups be necessary. The principal concept here is to promote and enable product champions from various business areas – that is, people who by virtue of their exposure to new developments and new ideas may be able to perceive new IT-related opportunities for their organisations.

Strong supplier relationships have been proved to produce superior results – not just in terms of the amount of function crammed into a system but in terms of overall corporate performance. A US study of the take-up and effects of videotext technology in banking, attributed strong supplier interaction as the only identifiable differential between the banks leading in the application of this technology and those who lagged (and were consequently losing market-share).

2 Maintain a Comprehensive Supply of Information Sources and Case Studies

Outside influences tend to have a far more significant effect on a company than those forces at work within it. IT is something which can be put to many and varied uses and no company has the monopoly on innovation and opportunism. It is vital that organisations are aware not just of pure technological developments, but also of how technology is being applied. In all the well-publicised competitive advantage case-studies it has been the application of the technology, rather that the presence of a particular technology in itself, which as provided the cutting edge. Whether you use the latest technical gizmo or not matters not one jot – providing that the technology that you do use has the basic capability to support the application.

Therefore, knowing your competitors are down-sizing their IT-environment, going over to Facilities Management or purchasing Relational Database software provides you with only limited demand-side facts. Knowing that they are launching new, IT-supported, customer services or products and the potential application of them to your business is valuable intelligence. Armed with this kind of information a strategic or tactical response can be made. Apart from forming the basis of a competitive intelligence program (which far too few companies operate – even in IT-driven sectors such as financial services) obtaining information on how IT is being used is a basic fuel for infopreneurial activity. Whether we term the process of technology transfer as 'lateral thinking' or 'thinking across boundaries', it is best demonstrated by examples from situations with which we are already familiar. In fact, lateral-thinking guru, Edward De Bono, actively promotes the study of examples as one of the best methods to encourage lateral thinking.

Therefore, provide individuals within your organisation with the ability to become intellectual plagiarists. There are many publications from both the specialist and general business press which carry details of IT applications. It is my experience that a week never goes by without a useful IT application being discussed somewhere. There is a wealth of information out there, provided that individuals within your organisation are motivated to go out and find it.

An article by Pamela Hammers Specht in the *American Journal of Small Business* entitled 'Information Sources Used for Strategic Planning Decisions in Small Firms' clearly demonstrated the power of continually harmonising a company's activities with its external environment:

A firm that can scan and react to trends in its external environment is most likely to succeed. The information itself is often personal or experience-based, rather than institutional, and this too appears to be significant in a changing, fluid business environment.

3 Initiate New Decision-Making, Tracking and Approval Processes

Becoming more responsive, accommodating changes and increasing innovation are goals that are shared by many, if not most, organisations today. From a general business perspective the attainment of these goals focuses on responses to external stimuli. IT is a factor in this of course, but also exerts considerable influence internally within a company. IT is capable of facilitating significant organisational and procedural change, but for this to happen those within the organisation must want change and actively seek it out.

Individuals need to be given the freedom to follow-up on 'hunches' and explore and conduct *ad hoc* research. Managers will need to adopt new methods of tracking progress as several mini-projects may be running concurrently within his area, in addition to day-to-day operations.

The principle that nothing is sacred should be the guiding light – particularly where information-intensive industries are concerned. Most procedures in organisations have been put into place to cope not with information *per se*, but with the medium on which it is recorded. The major attribute of IT is to provide a more effective means of recording and moving information, thereby creating the potential for radically different ways of working with information. However, the information that exists within many organisations often lies latent and unexploited because those with the detailed knowledge to exploit it are never encouraged to think about things differently. Consequently opportunities are lost.

To allow this environment to flourish managers will need to adopt the role of facilitators to allow employees more individual freedom in the following their ideas. It is now becoming generally accepted that the traditional management role of supervision and direction is dead and that leadership and facilitation form the predominant role. Encouraging and maintaining the direction of several infopreneurial projects, many of which will cross functional boundaries, will push this role to its limits.

Managers at all levels will need to acquire new skills of project evaluation (what is the potential here? What do I kill off to divert resources to IT?), resources allocation (how much time/resource should be devoted?) and project management (when should it be completed, how should we implement?). Neither will this be the only issue: while a company innovates for tomorrow, it must keep operating today. While infopreneurs are invaluable, they can be difficult to manage, consequently many managers do not bother. They leave the more difficult stuff associated with change to senior management and concentrate on keeping tomorrow much the same as today. While this approach makes life easier in the short term it is a death wish on opportunity and a recipe for mediocrity and lack of competitiveness.

4 Encourage Unstructured Information-Sharing

'Chinese Whispers', 'the Grapevine', etc., are often recognised as the most effective form of communication in any organisation. People tend to communicate more effectively in an informal manner than through formal channels for one very simple reason – they are less likely to be judged. So many of the systems evaluations I have seen are choc-full of caveats, where the writer tries to anticipate and minimise potential criticism. Ask the same person an IT-related question over the telephone and you generally get a straight answer.

Formal evaluations, reports, etc., have their place, but most organisations just do not have enough informal exchanges of information. A particularly good example of informal information-sharing (although I cannot condone the specific outcome of their efforts) are the electronic bulletin boards which have been (and still are) used by compute-hackers. Here the existence of a facility for informal and voluntary sharing of hints, tips and information on how to crack supposedly secure computer systems has provided enormous leverage to the hackers. With less than $1000 worth of equipment they have penetrated security systems which cost several hundred times more. The hacker is an archetypal infopreneur; one individual whose skill and knowledge is the sum of many other individuals' knowledge gained over time and channelled towards a finely tuned objective.

The issue is one of both knowledge and motivation – the motivation to achieve the objective drives the quest for knowledge, for all parties. Previously I said that all organisations should have an active supplier-liaison function for each software product actively used within it. They should also operate informal bulletin boards for each major software product in use. The provision of such a facility offers an immediate outlet for *ad hoc* questions and, as a useful by product, encourages widespread team work. E-Mail systems provide a superb vehicle for this and a fairly cheap method of doing it – particularly if you already have an E-Mail system in place.

These systems are not the place for disseminating formal documents such as proposals, requests for change and the like. Their function is to improve informal communication and promulgate knowledge and gems of wisdom throughout the organisation. This is the place to ask 'does anyone have a WP macro to ...?', 'did you know that using *xx* function of *ABC* system provides you with ...', 'has anybody tried ...?' and so on. So much useful knowledge about systems, their capabilities, features and the organisation in general is wasted because it is never disseminated throughout the organisation. Many organisations spend thousands if not millions relearning knowledge or duplicating activities which are already in place because they are simply unaware of their existence. The success of the hackers provides a sharp lesson in how knowledge-sharing can triumph over capital spending.

5 Know your Vertical Markets

'Vertical-market software' means software products which are specifically written for particular businesses such as legal practice, banks, real estate agency, etc.

In most industry sectors there are several if not dozens of suppliers providing packaged software for that particular sector or organisational function. Whilst each will do basically the same job, some do certain aspects better than others and some will run on different hardware/software platforms. Being aware of new product enhancements and general trends (connection to industry specific EDI networks for instances) is an important part of getting maximum value from IT.

By continually comparing the facilities available from various suppliers you are able to make substantive judgments about your own system, generate ideas for improvement and enhancement – and keep your current supplier on his toes! Too many organisations allow their systems to degenerate functionally by not being aware of what is going in the market.

This may seem unexciting and parochial but nonetheless current systems are often the best to build on – because they are the ones about which you know most. Notwithstanding the issues of technical obsolescence which may dictate replacement on the basis of costs and maintenance, building on the systems you have is generally cheaper and less risky than buying in new.

6 Always Use Multidisciplinary Teams

Never staff an evaluation or study team from one exclusive area of the organisation. Even though you might have hybrid managers or infopreneurs within the organisation, specialists have their role to play. Your infopreneurs/hybrid managers can play an important roles as arbiters and in maintaining overall balance, but the value of expert opinion should never be ignored.

When a particular technology or application is being evaluated, it is vital that both the technical and business implications are considered with equal tenacity. I have seen several projects in large organisations which have either failed to get off the ground or ended in dissatisfaction because the balance of skills within the evaluation team was too biased. One example of this was an evaluation of imaging technology undertaken by a large organisation where the evaluation team was staffed solely by technologists. The resulting evaluation was a superb technical evaluation of the pros, cons, performance and storage consideration of the technology – yet not one potential business application had been identified. Supplier price/performance comparisons and compatibility with existing systems are all vital information but are secondary until the value of the envisaged application has been perceived and established. Consequently the organisation was slow to take up the technology while several of its competitors were implementing image-based business systems.

Achieving the right skills balance in a team is crucial to its success. When an IT-related issue is being considered it is crucial that there is in-depth expertise in both the business issues and the technology issues to be addressed. The absence of this will result in one or the other being inadequately considered or completely overlooked.

7 Maintaining an Intra-Company Projects/Technology Database – 'Know What You Know'

It never ceases to amaze me how little is known – in large companies in particular – about what is going on in different areas of that company. Many organisations today have followed an evolutionary path of reorganising along the lines of strategic business units (SBUs) so as to allow focus on specific markets or products. This has been followed by a move toward decentralised IT whereby the business units have been given total control over their IT strategy, hardware/software procurement and development. The logic behind this cannot be denied and many organisations that have opted for this route have achieved a more responsive and focused IT department. However, there has been a downside to this which is that many of the SBUs have become introverted and consequently isolated from each other. Hence, valuable knowledge, experience and facilities that already exist within the company as a whole are lost.

I have seen instances in many decentralised companies where hundreds of thousands of pounds/dollars have been wasted because of duplication of effort and duplication of facilities which existed elsewhere in the organisation, albeit in a separate business unit. The following are just a few examples of this 'rogues gallery':

- Establishing contingency sites when similar sites have already been established.
- Retaining external consultants to advise on software which was already installed elsewhere.
- Buying in technicians on contract to undertake a systems implementation which had already been undertaken elsewhere.
- Evaluating technologies which have already been evaluated (and in some cases actually in use).
- Developing standards and procedures that already exist.

This list could probably fill a book and if it did not represent millions of wasted cash, it might even be faintly amusing. The French philosopher, Descartes, mused on the problem 'How do we know what we know?' From an organisational perspective, this question could be framed slightly differently by asking 'How do organisations know what they know?' The answer is, of course, far too many are not aware of the knowledge and expertise that exists within them – simply because there is no repository for it.

Barely a week goes by without some mention in the trade or national press of the impending skills shortage or the need to become a learning organisation. Yet many companies exacerbate this problem for themselves because of poor internal communication. An intra-company database of technology projects, technology evaluations, individuals who have participated in them, individuals who have a particular expertise in a certain system or experience of systems for a particular application is an important step in the right direction. A central, easily accessible repository of IT experience and expertise not only allows you to 'know what you know', it forms the foundation for the informal information-sharing mentioned earlier and promotes the growth of informal networks throughout the organisation.

A final more general point is that this approach will, I believe, become a more general management tool. As the need to capitalise on the existence of specialist skills increases and the availability of 'traditional' career paths continues to decrease, organisations will have to become more adept at managing the skills available to them. By using the approach of a skill-and-experience database, organisations will be better enabled to identify and locate such skills and effectively deploy them.

8 Encourage Experimentation – 'Nothing Succeeds like Failure'

There is one thing that is common in any IT project or initiative: no one knows how it will turn out. Regardless of what methodologies, techniques or forecasting approaches are used, the only certain thing is that there will be uncertainty. No one can guarantee that the envisaged benefits can actually be achieved or that the project will be completed by the proposed delivery date.

Many 'critical' projects suffer because of this universal truth. One of the major reasons is because organisations try too much too soon. Consequently, the amount of capital (and reputations) invested in a project become so large that failure cannot be contemplated. Yet if the project were to start in a small way, it would probably be canned. When large projects start to get out of control, the organisation goes into damage-limitation mode, learning stops, motivation decreases and the general attitude becomes 'implement something at any cost'.

One of the most crucial aspects in effectively deploying and exploiting IT is that of confidence – confidence in the outcome. The more familiar you are with the components of a given initiative, the more confident you can be of the eventual results.

When putting IT to use in new areas or in adopting new IT products organisations should adopt two guiding principles:

- start small;
- tolerate failure.

Start Small. Trying an idea is the best way of seeing if it will work. Trying it on your whole customer base, switching over to a new system overnight, however, is a recipe for disaster. Keep new systems initiatives small and conduct pilots.

The small-step approach confers several advantages. First, the project becomes manageable even when there is sparse knowledge. Low financial commitments correspond to low risk and hence failure is not equivalent to disaster. In addition there is less pressure on those involved with the project to make it work at any cost. Smaller projects which are not (yet) mission-critical from a business perspective can be evaluated from a substantive viewpoint. If the future of the organisation is not hanging in the balance there will be less pressure to continue should the assumptions about the application or the technology prove incorrect. Likewise those involved are likely to learn from their mistakes and be in a position to make judgments as to whether a large-scale development is worthwhile or desirable.

Instigating a small pilot scheme allows you to fail and provides a far superior basis for evaluation than the mega-project with 'all your eggs in one basket'.

Tolerate Failure. Declaring that an idea will not provide the benefits envisaged, based on a small-start, pilot-project, is not failure – it is successful risk management.

In his book, *Managing in Turbulent Times,* Peter Drucker introduced the concept of a manager's 'batting average'. The concept is that there is a ratio of successful initiatives to total initiatives taken by management of around 0.3. Which implies that only 30 per cent of management's ideas bear fruit. If the successes compensate for the failures, then it must follow that the more initiatives are taken then the more successes are likely.

IT is no different – you have to keep trying to succeed. The more you try the more you succeed even if at first you fail. The key to the equation is to tolerate failure by making failures tolerable. Failure is made tolerable by small investments in small starts which encourage learning and evaluation – not mega-projects which require salvaging at any cost.

9 Ensure Reward Systems are Commensurate with Contribution and Proficiency

While most organisations recognise and often articulate the importance of effective information management, those that actually do anything to encourage it are rarer than a hen's teeth. To encourage those within the organisation to exploit information as an integral part of their job, particularly when 'computers' are not the core function of their work, requires that exploiting information is made worthwhile. Most performance-management systems measure things such as interpersonal skills and vocational effectiveness. However, as the exploitation of the capabilities of IT become more and more important to organisational effectiveness, an individual's ability to exploit the use of information via IT will become just as important. 'Information effectiveness' is an attribute which will become just as important as the myriad of other skills which a person must posses in order to further his/her career progression.

From the organisation's perspective the absence of any kind of system to recognise, reward and develop its infopreneurs, denies that organisation a critical resource. By failing to recognise the infopreneurs within it, an organisation denies itself and those within it. Both opportunities and skills will be lost.

Only a handful of organisations actually have any kind of assessment of IT-proficiency within their appraisal or performance-management systems. Sadly, those that do are looking at the situation through a flawed perspective. As mentioned previously most skills measurement, whether they be interpersonal or professional, tend to be measured in their vocational context – for instance 'the skills of *XYZ* denote a good accountant'. IT-proficiency, in those companies that are trying to measure it, is measured on the same basis. That is, they will try to assess whether a person is expert or not in terms of their level of experience, thus categorising people as 'expert' users or technologists. But it does not matter one jot whether you have been on the periphery of IT-application for the past twenty years or not. What really makes the difference is the knowledge of the capabilities of IT, a thirst for more knowledge, the motivation to learn more and the plain old-fashioned ability to come up with some new ideas.

In my experience this type of proficiency with IT is not measured on a personal level. Consequently, because organisations do not look for it, they have not a clue as to how much of it is lying latent within their organisations. Herein lies probably the most significant aspect of exploiting information technology. If we accept that exploiting IT is enabled by lateral thinking, thinking across boundaries or whatever else you may wish to call it, then we must accept that the use of IT in an organisation will be best advanced by those who are capable of identifying new, extended and innovative solutions for it. Yet we have no way of identifying who those individuals are.

First, to capitalise fully on the talent within them, organisations will need to adopt new appraisal categories within their performance-management systems. They must first incorporate both formal and informal techniques to recognise infopreneurs.

Second, they need to determine assessment criteria to evaluate their infopreneurial capability, proficiency and potential. Thirdly, and probably most importantly as this will be the sustaining force which will continue to encourage infopreneurship, there must be a reward system to provide the motivation to be and keep on being an infopreneur.

In terms of evaluating an infopreneur, measuring or evaluating technical proficiency (either as a user, developer or supporter) is simply not enough. The ability to envisage new uses and opportunities is arguably more important than technical proficiency. For it is this ability to see an opportunity which is the forerunner and genesis of IT-led innovation. Although technical and managerial skills are required to implement a given initiative, without the vision and perspective there is no guiding light to apply these implementative skills.

In the future individuals at all levels will need to be evaluated on a far broader and more sophisticated basis than before – at least with respect to their ability to manage information. In addition to their technical, managerial and business proficiency, their aptitudes for dealing with information must also be evaluated in terms of:

- The ability to identify work related improvements by the use of information technology.
- Their ability to understand the capabilities and potential application of new technologies.
- The knowledge (or level of competitive intelligence) regarding the business implications of competitors IT initiatives.
- The number of IT oriented suggestions they come up with.
- Their role in disseminating IT related knowledge to other areas of the organisation.

Most organisations know that information and IT are crucial factors in growth and survival. Very few, however, are doing anything to achieve that aim by unlocking and enabling those catalysts that exist within them.

The precise emoluments which may be extended to an above-average infopreneur may vary. The overwhelming principle, though, does not. Infopreneurs may not be above-average line or project managers and may not even be very good at implementing their ideas when it gets down to the nitty-gritty of installation. They may not be aspiring CEOs. They may get their kicks from research and subsequent influence rather that their position in the corporate hierarchy. As performance-management systems must change in order to recognise an infopreneur, so reward systems must change in order to reward and encourage subsequent infopreneurship.

Most people are driven by two basic principles at work, once the primary requirements of survival and security have been met. These may be categorised into job satisfaction (although how that it achieved is highly individualistic) and reward – which is generally measured in financial terms or some other form of differentiation. To provide a reward system for infopreneurs some of the following may provide the necessary motivations and encouragement:

- Make one-off payments or bonuses for *ad hoc* initiatives. For instance, designing, writing or identifying a useful WP macro, spreadsheet template or database query that has application elsewhere in the organisation.
- An IT applications suggestion scheme with payments.
- Being chosen as a company envoy to visit trade shows.
- Admission to company-sponsored high-profile training/ education schemes.
- Being allowed to act as an internal consultant for several months.
- A visit to major suppliers to be briefed on their strategy and new products.

These are only a few of the rewards an organisation may choose to bestow upon its infopreneurs – there are many others that might be appropriate. The exact nature of the reward system and the prizes bestowed by it are less important than the principles on which it is founded. These principles should remain firmly focused on maintaining a continuing motivation to seek out IT-supported opportunities to improve personal and organisational performance.

10 Ensure that IT Training is Given in a Work-Related Context

IT-related training courses are more notable for their sheer number than for their value to those who attend them. The vast majority of IT-related training courses concern themselves with technical orientation issues, rather than showing those attending these courses how they can work more productively or effectively by using the technology. The general inference appears to be that by understanding the principles of operation and a number of commands, then exploitation of the technology in a work-related context will follow as a natural consequence. Nothing, in fact, could be further from the truth.

My own experience with end-user training, whether it is the utilitarian PC-orientation training or training given prior to implementing a new application system, is that the users spend the majority of their efforts merely coping with the system in question. The next stage is gaining some idea of how they might conduct the simpler aspects of their job using the new tools. but exploitation, changing the way they work, is way off in the wild blue yonder. The problem is the contextual nature of most training courses. The majority of end-user training is directed towards teaching users to interact with systems at the *command level* rather than the *outcome level.*

Command level training is about teaching a user what buttons to press and what instructions to submit in order to work a particular feature of a certain package. The *outcome level of training* is both more holistic and more orientated towards achieving a particular result within a specific context. The situation is analogous to planning a journey. Say you wanted to go from London to Scotland, making three or four stops on the way and decide to pop into your local auto-club for some advice. The first person you ask gives you a comprehensive lecture on all the motorways in Great Britain, whether they run north to south or east to west, how many services they have, their names, how many exits there are and the further possible routes which you can take from each exit. The next person you ask enquires where you are starting, where you want to go, how much time you have and what time you wish to arrive. You are then furnished with the following information:

- how to get from your starting-point to the motorway;
- what particular exits to take in order to reach your stop-over locations;

- how to get back on the motorway from your stop-over;
- details of services which fall in between the exits in which you are interested and which might be useful refreshment stops.

Who has provided the most useful information? No contest, is there? The first person bombarded your with facts but did nothing to increase your knowledge. The second person gave you instructions that were relevant to your requirements and in the context of something with which you are already familiar.

The problem with so much end-user IT-training (and particularly that related to PC training) is that it falls in the former category. It sets out to instruct people how to command each and every function of a package – whether it is relevant to their job or not. Consequently the trainees are bombarded with instruction but provided with little useful tuition on how to employ those features that are relevant to them.

Does this imply that more vocationally-oriented training will be the order of the day – YES it does. Suppliers of IT-products and independent trainers will have to provide far more specific training; products and organisations will have to be prepared for their employees not only to be trained more but refreshed more frequently. We have reflected in earlier chapters on the way that the ever-increasing power and sophistication of IT is making information more versatile. With this versatility however comes a plethora of choices and abstraction. For instance, relational databases via their query languages were intended to liberate users by providing easy access to information. However, many users found the concepts of relational databases difficult to deal with – even though they knew what buttons to press on the keyboard. Others simply did not know what information was held within the database or its relevance to them. Consequently, in order to facilitate both learning and conceptual understanding of the potential use of technology, the training of IT-concepts must be given in a manner which is contextually familiar to the recipient.

EXECUTIVE SECRETARY'S DAY THURSDAY, 10-4 ... STOP BY

THE APPLE® SEMINAR SERIES

The most profitable few hours you'll ever spend out of the office.

The seminars are free — and no previous Macintosh® experience is required. A knowledgeable Macintosh expert will demonstrate how this powerful and versatile computer can be put to work right now in your organization — no matter what business or computer environment you work in.

If you'd like to reserve your place at one of our seminars shown at right just call the number below.

1-800-944-9628, ext. 806

You can call 7 days a week, 24 hours a day. But spaces are limited, so you should call right away.

©1992 Apple Computer, Inc. Apple, the Apple logo and Macintosh are registered trademarks of Apple Computer, Inc.

All Seminars will be held in New York City.

SEMINAR	DATE	TIME	SPONSOR
DTP, PRESENTATIONS & MULTIMEDIA			
Color PrePress: What the Macintosh Can Do	9/9	10 AM - 1 PM	MicroComputer Publishing Center
Desktop Video: The Ultimate Business Communication	9/11	9 - 11, 1 - 3	Microcomputer Publishing Center
Macintosh: The Power Color Publishing solution	9/14	9 - 11, 1 - 3	Essex Computers
Publishing MultiMedia & Information on CD Rom	9/16	10 AM - 1 PM	Apple Computer, Inc.
Choosing a Desktop Publishing System	9/17	10 - 1, 2 - 5	Apple Computer, Inc.
Affordable Video Production on the Macintosh	9/22	10 AM - 1 PM	Apple Computer, Inc.
Advertising: Increase Sales with Macintosh	9/23	10 AM - 12 PM	Apple Computer, Inc.
How do I use MultiMedia for my work?	9/25	10 AM - 1 PM	Apple Computer, Inc.
Scanning and Digital Retouching on Your Macintosh	9/30	10 AM - 1 PM	MicroComputer Publishing Center
LEGAL			
Law Office Automation with Macintosh	9/15	5:30 PM - 7:30 PM	Apple Computer, Inc.
Litigation and Case Management	9/24	5:30 PM - 7:30 PM	Apple Computer, Inc.
On Line Research	9/24	4 PM - 5 PM	Apple Computer, Inc.
BUSINESS PRODUCTIVITY			
Retail Store of the Future	8/31, 9/14, 9/29	10 AM - 1 PM	Apple Computer, Inc
Easy Ways to Market your Business w/Easy-To-Use Technology	9/2	10 - 12, 2 - 4	Intelligent Electronics
Facilities Management with Macintosh	9/15	10 AM - 12 PM	Apple Computer, Inc.
Fashion: Retail Store Solutions	9/15	10 - 12, 1 - 3	Apple Computer, Inc.
Choosing a Macintosh for Public Relations	9/16	10 - 12, 1 - 3	Apple Computer, Inc.
PowerBook: The Mobile Office	9/23	10 AM - 1 PM	Apple Computer, Inc.
Small Business Productivity Tools	9/25	1 PM - 3 PM	Apple Computer, Inc.
Taking your Business Into Account with Macintosh	9/25	1 PM - 3 PM	Apple Computer, Inc.
THE BASICS			
Getting the Most out of Microsoft Excel and Lotus 1,2,3	8/31, 9/10	10 AM - 1 PM	Computer Era
Macintosh: Try it Before You Buy It	9/3, 9/30	10 - 12, 1 - 3	Apple Computer, Inc.
Accounting for Retail Business	9/11	2 PM - 4 PM	Apple Computer, Inc.
Choosing a Macintosh for Your Business	9/11	10 AM - 1 PM	Apple Computer, Inc.
Buying a Mac IIsi, IIci, or Quadra	9/16	10 AM - 1 PM	Apple Computer, Inc.
Getting the Most out of your Macintosh Network	9/17	10 AM - 1 PM	Computer Era
Choosing a Macintosh for Your Business	9/18	1 PM - 4 PM	Apple Computer, Inc.
DESIGN & MANUFACTURING			
Open House for Executive Secretaries	8/27	10 AM - 4 PM	Apple Computer, Inc.
Macintosh Rendering Tools	9/18	10 AM - 1 PM	Apple Computer, Inc.
Macintosh for Textile Design	9/23	10 AM - 1 PM	Apple Computer, Inc.
The Power of CAD with the Ease of Macintosh	9/25	10 AM - 1 PM	Apple Computer, Inc.
ACCOUNTING			
Accounting for Advertising & Graphic Design	9/1	10 AM - 12 PM	Apple Computer, Inc.
Accounting for Advertising & Graphic Design	9/15	1:30 PM - 3:30 PM	Apple Computer, Inc.
Choosing a Macintosh to Create Catalogues	9/15	10 AM - 1 PM	Apple Computer, Inc.
Choosing Accounting for Wholesale Distribution	9/15	1 PM - 3 PM	Apple Computer, Inc.
Choosing Small Business Accounting Solutions	9/15	10 AM - 1 PM	Apple Computer, Inc.
Time Billing & Accounting for the Law Office	9/15	4 PM - 5 PM	Apple Computer, Inc.
Accounting for Architecture and Construction	9/22	1 PM - 3 PM	Apple Computer, Inc.
Time Billing & Accounting for the Law Office	9/24	1 PM - 3 PM	Apple Computer, Inc.
NETWORKING & COMMUNICATIONS			
Intro to Networking in a Macintosh Environment	8/28	10 AM - 1 PM	Apple Computer, Inc.
Mac to DOS : Making the Connection	9/9	10 AM - 1 PM	Apple Computer, Inc.
Macintosh Network Management Strategies for the '90s	9/18	10 AM - 1 PM	Apple Computer, Inc.
Macintosh to Sun (Unix)	9/18	10 AM - 1 PM	Custom Computer Specialists
HEALTHCARE			
Dental Office Automation on the Mac Integrated with Intraoral & Extraoral Imaging, Voice Activated Charting & MultiMedia Word Processing	9/17	1 PM - 3 PM	Apple Computer, Inc.
Medical Office Automation on the Macintosh	9/17	9 AM - 12 PM	Apple Computer, Inc.
Psychotherapy Office Management with Macintosh	9/22	10 AM - 12 PM	Apple Computer, Inc.
MULTILINGUAL			
Multi-Lingual Computing with Macintosh	9/16	1 PM - 3 PM	Apple Computer, Inc.
La Oficina Creativa	9/22	2 PM - 4 PM	Apple Computer, Inc.
Selecionando Un Macintosh Para Su Negocio	9/22	10 AM - 1 PM	Apple Computer, Inc.
Kanji Solutions: Macintosh Open House	9/29	11 AM - 2 PM	Apple Computer, Inc.

Some moves are being made in the right direction. The above illustration is a reprint of a recent advertisement which appeared in the *New York Times* for Apple Computer. Notice how specific to particular types of business, some of the courses are. Apple has recognised that the sheer comprehensiveness of its systems provides that end-user with an overwhelming battery of choices. No matter how many icons you use, this does not necessarily ensure that the end-user will understand *how* particular features will provide a benefit to him or her.

Apple's focus on the end-user has enabled it to edge ahead of other suppliers in this respect – but they will all have to follow suit. As IT-products become more versatile, so more instruction will have to be given on how to achieve desired results.

In the longer term the need to give a vocational or contextual perspective on IT will require changes in the educational system at all levels. Children will need to be educated in using IT to complete assignments in other subjects such as mathematics, history, biology, etc. Students and those studying for professional examinations in particular will have to know how IT is used within a particular profession such as marketing, accounting, engineering or design. Teaching IT as a generalised subject in itself will have only limited use. The real issue is training people in how to deal effectively with, and process, information which is relevant to their vocational activities.

11 Ensuring that Business Vision and Commercial Objectives are Clearly Communicated

The real issue with communicating a business vision is not telling those within the organisation what it is – most large organisations have several employee communications programs that serve as the vehicle for communicating this. The real issue is that of making the message meaningful so that those receiving it can relate their own area of activity to the overall picture. Unfortunately too many business visions are far too nebulous for this personalisation to occur. Statements such as being 'the premier in the industry', 'the leader in customer service' or 'maximising shareholder value' are fine and laudable ideals. But precisely what they mean in terms of day-to-day operations – who knows? How does a bank teller personalise 'maximising shareholder value' in his/her daily activities? If the message is so vague as to defy translation into one or several actions which would result in an appropriate measurable outcome, no supporting system can be defined.

Strong corporate messages do make a difference. The case of Federal Express, the American parcels carrier is a good example. The business vision and objective from CEO Fred Smith was simple 'We want every parcel on our customers' desks by 10 a.m. the next morning'. Simple and effective. Rather than the bland 'leader in customer service' a simple, clear and unambiguous statement spelt it out. The 'by 10 a.m.' message was a powerful focus for every employee in the organisation. It gave them all the information they needed to determine how they would have to change to achieve this aim and a reference point on which to evaluate all forthcoming initiatives. The Federal Express company focused their efforts on fast delivery by quantum-leap improvements in the speed with which information flowed through the company and to its customers. At the heart of this was the COSMOS system which continually tracks the progress of each individual parcel. There can be no argument here that at Federal Express their business and IT-strategies are closely aligned, in fact, they are so closely harmonised it is difficult to see where one ends and the other begins.

For any business vision to be understood to the point where an operational response can be understood, it must contain an 'organising principle', a message that says 'This is what we are here to do'. Although the precise 'how' of this response may not be within the CEO's office the message becomes clear enough for line departments and divisions to understand the operational implications. By communicating a vision in these terms the role of support systems becomes easier to establish. Again, consider Federal Express: its systems investments were focused on enabling the by 10 a.m. objective. Federal Express knew that 'superior customer service' meant fast reliable delivery and that fast reliable delivery attracted and retained customers, and from customers your derive revenue. What, though, would have happened at Federal Express if Fred Smith's message had been 'To achieve consistent revenue growth'. Not very much; it is such a bland statement that it is difficult to derive any organising principle from it and thus any systems which might support it. Probably very little would have changed in the way Federal Express operates such a statement would more likely have sparked off cost-cutting exercises, fixation with financial ratios and the use of IT for labour cost substitution projects.

12 Instigate an Appraisal System for Infopreneurs

If you want to encourage infopreneurship within your organisation, one of the best ways to do this is to demonstrate that being an infopreneur is worthwhile. Therefore, within your firm's current performance-management system, you should include some assessment of an individual's infopreneurial capability. By recognising certain attributes it is possible to gain some insight into an individual's ability to envisage new and extended use of IT.

Assessment of the following principles will provide an overall guide to a particular individual's aptitude:

- Does the person often find IT-supported solutions to business/organisational problems?
- Does he/she demonstrate a keen awareness of the current and future capabilities of systems within their sphere of operation?
- Does he/she make extensive use of internal and external information services?
- Does he/she extend his/her own personal use of IT (i.e. have more software on PC than anyone else, does he/she insist on having a portable PC?)
- Does the person extend his/her use of IT beyond that of other colleagues, for instance, by creating personal database, having access to more systems?
- Does he/she actively seek out new IT-related skills by following tutorials during lunch hour/after work?
- Does the person submit unsolicited proposals (either written or verbal) for new ways of using existing systems?
- Do other colleagues consider the person to be especially knowledgable?

- Is he/she keen to learn new technologies and their potential application?
- Does his/her choice of training courses indicate a desire to extend his/her knowledge (as opposed to confirming his/her current knowledge base)?

13 Dissipate the IT Function throughout the Organisation

In the *1991 IT Review,* conducted by Price Waterhouse, the main concern of the majority of IT Managers was the 'culture gap'. Fundamentally, this relates to an IT-person developing an empathy with the issue with which his users have to deal and vice versa. It is seen as a major reason why IT-practitioners fail to understand the business and IT systems fail to deliver the required benefits. The problem lies in closing this culture gap.

Now, let us pose a hypothetical question. If it was necessary for an individual to understand the cultural differences between his native country and another, what would be the best way of doing this? Would it be reading about it, attending seminars or watching videos about it, or, perhaps going to live in that country for a while? If your answer is anything other than the last, I would be amazed. It is obvious, really, because it is the personal experience that will make the greatest impression and create the greater empathy.

It is time for IT to come out of its ivory tower and become part of the organisation it seeks to serve. The IT department should start seconding its staff to business units for extended periods. Sending an IT person to a user department for a week just to 'see what they do' simply will not help. They have to become part of that department – part of their culture, before any empathy can be developed.

This need not mean that the IT staff have no meaningful work to do during the period of secondment. Undertaking a large mission-critical project whilst at the same time significantly changing the structure of the IT department is a high-risk approach. But maintenance and enhancement of current systems could be done under this scenario. Thus a member of the IT department could undertake systems maintenance and enhancement duties within the physical locale of the user department. This immediately breaks down one enormous psychological barrier – departmental boundaries. The long-term physical presence of IT-development activity within the user department will familiarise users with IT, and remove some of its mystery.

One of the greatest barriers to exploiting IT for the benefit of the business is being unable to see across the boundary of the two apparently unrelated disciplines. By integrating IT-staff with user departments on an ongoing day-to-day basis, these boundaries are at least moved closer together.

14 Tell Them What's Important

Let your infopreneurs know what the important things are in your business. Tell them what information you need to 'feel the pulse' of the business, what things *must* go right for the business to succeed. Provide them with corporate intelligence – for instance, what areas must be improved in order to increase competitiveness, improve customer service, reduce distribution costs or manage risks more effectively. Nothing focuses an infopreneur's mind more than a problem, particularly if it is a significant business issue.

The real key to obtaining value for IT is that it is deployed in activities that are of significant importance to the company. Let your infopreneurs know what these issues are, talk to them about the problems of the business and then set them to work. Be prepared also to spend some time talking about the business, its problems and where it might be going. All these things are important in providing a focus on the right things, rather than periphery, non-value adding issues. You do not need to tell your infopreneurs *how* to do it – just what is important to the business.

Most organisations will acknowledge that at least some of the suggestions mentioned here are in place and make little if any appreciable difference to the way in which IT contributes to the overall performance of the organisation. Likewise many organisations could pick up one of the many books on how to be an 'excellent' company and could also confirm that some of the suggested systems and techniques are already in place – but seem to make no difference.

Underlying the initiatives previously outlined are two subtle aspects which are crucial to success. An attitude of 'do this and then everything will be fine' will not achieve the goal. As with any initiative which ultimately relies on employees to take the necessary steps there has to be a management 'buy-in' at all levels. There must be a genuine desire not only for a better bottom line but a sincere wish to serve customers better, because there is a real sense of pride in doing so. Management must want to give employees greater scope and more rewarding jobs, not just because firms which do these things seem to make more money, but because they genuinely want their firm to be a better place in which to work.

Bibliography

BONOMA, T., *The Marketing Edge: Making Strategies Work* (New York: Free Press, 1985)

BUTLER, D., 'Information Technology and Realpolitik', in *Butler Cox Foundation* (1986).

BUTLER COX FOUNDATION SURVEY, 1986, *Butler Cox Foundation* (1986).

CECIL, J. and GOLDSTEIN, M., 'Sustaining Competitive Advantage From IT', *McKinsey Quarterly*, no 4, 1990.

DRUCKER, P., *Managing in Turbulent Times* (New York: Harper & Row, 1980).

GARDNER, M., 'Aha! Insight', *The Scientific American* (1987).

GILB, T., *Principles of Software Engineering Management* (Addison-Wesley, 1988).

GOOLD, M. and CAMPBELL, A., *Strategies and Styles* (Oxford: Blackwell, 1990).

HAMMERS-SPRECHT, P., 'Information Sources Used For Strategic Planning Decisions in Small Firms' *American Journal of Small Business* (Spring, 1987).

HANDY, C., *Understanding Organisations* (Harmondsworth: Penguin, 1985).

HASTINGS, C., BIXBY, P., and CHAUDHRY-LAWTON, R., *Superteams* (London: Fontana, 1986).

IVES, B. and LEARMOUTH, G., 'The Information System As A Competitive Weapon', *Communications of the Association of Computer Manufacturers* (December 1984).

NAISBITT, J., *Megatrends* (New York: Warner Books Inc., 1982)

PETERS, T., *Thriving On Chaos* (London: Macmillan, 1988).

PETERS, T. and WATERMAN, R., *In Search of Excellence* (New York: Harper & Row, 1982).

PORTER, M., *Competitive Strategy: Techniques for Analysing Industries and Competitors* (New York: Free Press, 1980).

PORTER, M., *Competitive Advantage: Creating and Sustaining Superior Performance* (New York: Free Press, 1985).

PRICE WATERHOUSE, *PW/Computing Review, 1991* (1991).

STRASSMAN, P., *Information Payoff* (New York: Free Press, 1985).

WHIPP, R., 'Managing Technological Changes: Opportunities and Pitfalls', *International Journal of Vehicle Design.* XII, nos 5–6 (1991).

ZUBOFF, Prof. S. *The Age of the Smart Machine* (New York: Basic Books Inc., 1988).

Index